The first step to becoming a Master of the Tarot: Pick the right deck

Traditional decks ... cross-cultural decks ... nature-based decks ... abstract decks ... decks with numbers ... decks with lavish illustrations ... decks by famous artists ... decks by unknowns. Every deck has its own unique spin on the symbolism and art of this ancient occult tool. Finally, a handy guidebook—written by a renowned scholar of the esoteric—has come along to take the mystery out this daunting selection.

Different decks are better for different purposes. Most people are familiar with the Tarot's use as a fortunetelling device, a legitimate aim that is dealt with at length in this book. But the Tarot is also used for meditation, astral journeys, and magick. A deck that is invaluable for divination may be too distracting for pathworking. A deck suited for magical workings may not be useful in meditations. In many cases, two or three decks may be required.

This thorough introduction to the subject includes a chapter on the Tarot's history, as well as how-to chapters on divination, meditation, pathworking, dreamworking, magick, and collecting.

About the Author

David Godwin was born in Dallas, Texas, and is a former resident of Houston, Atlanta, Miami, and New York. He has a Bachelor of Journalism degree from the University of Texas. He is currently Senior Editor at Llewellyn Publications and lives in Lakeville, Minnesota, with two dogs, six cats, and an editor.

To Write to the Author

If you wish to contact the author or would like more information about this book, please write to the author in care of Llewellyn Worldwide and we will forward your request. Both the author and publisher appreciate hearing from you and learning of your enjoyment of this book and how it has helped you. Llewellyn Worldwide cannot guarantee that every letter written to the author can be answered, but all will be forwarded. Please write to:

David Godwin
c/o Llewellyn Worldwide
P.O. Box 64383-K323, St. Paul, MN 55164-0383,
U.S.A.

Please enclose a self-addressed, stamped envelope for reply, or $1.00 to cover costs.

If outside U.S.A., enclose international postal reply coupon.

Free Catalog from Llewellyn

For more than 90 years Llewellyn has brought its readers knowledge in the fields of metaphysics and human potential. Learn about the newest books in spiritual guidance, natural healing, astrology, occult philosophy and more. Enjoy book reviews, new age articles, a calendar of events, plus current advertised products and services. To get your free copy of the *Llewellyn's New Worlds of Mind and Spirit*, write to:

Llewellyn's New Worlds of Mind and Spirit
P.O. Box 64383-K323, St. Paul, MN 55164-0383,
U.S.A.

Llewellyn's How-to Series

How to Choose Your Own Tarot

David Godwin

1995
Llewellyn Publications
St. Paul, Minnesota 55164-0383, U.S.A.

FIRST EDITION
First Printing, 1995

Cover design by Lynne Menterweck
Cover illustration by Anne Marie Garrison
Interior design and editing by David Godwin and Laura Gudbaur
Rider-Waite Tarot card illustrations reproduced from the designs by Pamela Colman Smith in the 1922 reprint of the original 1910 edition of *The Pictorial Key to the Tarot* by Arthur Edward Waite, William Rider & Son Ltd., London.
Other decks included: *Witches Tarot* by Ellen Cannon Reed and Martin Cannon, *The New Golden Dawn Ritual Tarot Deck* by Sandra Tabatha Cicero, *The Tarot of the Orishas* by Zolrak, *Legend: The Arthurian Tarot* by Anna Marie Ferguson, *The Healing Earth Tarot* by Jyoti and David McKie, all of Llewellyn Publications.

Cataloging-in-Publication Data
Godwin, David.
    How to choose your own tarot/ David Godwin. 1st ed.
        p. cm. -- (Llewellyn's vanguard series)
    ISBN 1-56718-323-9
1. Tarot. 2. Fortune-telling by cards. 3. Divination I. Title. II. Series
BF1879. T2G63 1995   95-2735
                                             CIP
133.3'2424--dc20

Llewellyn Publications
A Division of Llewellyn Worldwide, Ltd.
P.O. Box 64383, St. Paul, MN 55164-0383

HOW TO DO IT!

No matter what it is, the important question always is: "How to do it?"

The mind has many marvelous powers—far more than you have ever dreamed of—and humanity has barely begun the wonderful evolutionary journey that will let us tap into them all at will. We grow in our abilities as we do things.

There are many wonderful things you can do. As you do them, you learn more about the innate qualities of mind and spirit, and as you exercise these inner abilities, they will grow in strength—as will your vision of your mental and spiritual potential.

In learning to *Choose Your Own Tarot Deck*, or making a *Love Charm* or using a *Magic Mirror*, or many other strange and wonderful things, you are extending—just a little bit—the tremendous gift that lies within, the Life Force itself.

We are born that we may grow, and not to use this gift—not to grow in your perception and understanding of it—is to turn away from the gifts of Life, of Love, of Beauty, of Happiness that are the very reason for Creation.

Learning how to do these things is to open psychic windows to New Worlds of Mind & Spirit. Actually doing these things is to enter New Worlds. Each of these things that we do is a step forward in accepting responsibility for the worlds that you can shape and influence.

Simple, easy to follow, yet so very rewarding. Following these step-by-step instructions can start you upon high adventure. Gain control over the world around you, and step into *New Worlds of Mind & Spirit*.

Other Books by David Godwin

Godwin's Cabalistic Encyclopedia

Light in Extension:
   Greek Magic from Homer to Modern Times

The Truth About Cabala

This one is for Julius, Rusty,
Abby, Auriel, and T.T. Punk

Contents

❧ 1 ❧

What Is the Tarot

The Tarot is a deck of 78 cards. It is divided into a Major Arcana of 22 cards, also called the Trumps or Keys, and a Minor Arcana of 56 cards. "Arcana" is the plural of "arcanum" and means a mystery or secret. The term was first applied to the Tarot in the nineteenth century by French occultists, who were the first we know of to see an esoteric meaning in the cards. Before that, they were just a deck of cards with an exceptional number of Trumps, although they were apparently used for divination by such groups as the Romany, also known as the Gypsies. Modern playing cards evolved from the Tarot, and these are also used as a divinatory tool by the same groups.

In esoteric thought, the cards of the Major Arcana—that is, the Trumps—are considered to be much more important than the other cards. Unlike the lesser cards (until modern times), the Trumps were illustrated with scenes and figures which are now thought to be of archetypal significance, speaking directly to the subconscious mind. The cards thus have an effect on the psyche of anyone who spends any time looking at them, even if it is not intended by the one doing the looking. More than that, the Trumps are thought to have magical and spiritual significance.

All that remains of the Major Arcana in a modern deck of cards used for bridge, poker, and so forth is the Joker, the counterpart of the Fool of the Tarot.

The Minor Arcana of 56 cards consists of four suits of 14 cards each—ten numbered cards (including the Ace) and four court cards. The court cards are usually called King, Queen, Knight, and Page, although some decks use other names such as Prince, Princess, Knave, and so on.

The suits of a modern deck of cards— spades, hearts, diamonds, and clubs—are derived from the older Tarot suits: Swords, Cups, Coins, and Staves. In modern decks, Coins are usually called Pentacles and Staves are generally called Wands. This arrangement was adopted to conform more agreeably with the four elemental weapons of a ceremonial magician of the Hermetic Order of the Golden Dawn:

Four of Cups from the New Golden Dawn Ritual Tarot

Nine of Cups from the Rider/Waite Tarot

the Dagger for Air, the Cup for Water, the Pentacle for Earth, and the Wand for Fire.

It is no coincidence that the suits of the modern Tarot follow this pattern, because this terminology was first used in the Tarot deck designed by A.E. Waite, a member and leader of the Golden Dawn. The cards were drawn by Pamela Colman Smith, and published by Rider & Co. in London in 1910—the so-called Rider/Waite deck. Aside from cards published for the purpose of game-playing, this was the first widespread publication of the Tarot, and almost all subsequent decks have followed its pattern or have at least been heavily influenced by it.

Older decks do not have illustrations on the numbered cards, but simply bear the appropriate number of objects. The Nine of Cups, for example, just shows nine cups. Waite, however, decided to put a thematic illustration on each card—for example, a self-satisfied fat man sitting with his arms folded and nine empty cups on a curved counter behind him, illustrating the divinatory meaning of material happiness. This tradition has been followed in quite a few modern decks.

Most people who know about the existence of the Tarot think of it as a fortunetelling device; i.e., an instrument to be used for divination. This is a legitimate use of the cards and will be dealt with at length in this book. However, the cards are not limited to this function. Their oldest and simplest use is in card games, just as modern playing cards are used. Aside from that, they may also be used for meditation, astral journeys, magic, or the rather more mundane use as collector's items, for their esthetic appeal, quite apart from any occult or mystical significance they may have or claim to have.

Selecting a Tarot deck is the topic of this book—helping you to sort out the confusion as to which deck to use. Most dealers in specialty bookshops will tell you to simply pick a deck that "feels right to you," and this is good advice. But it ignores the fact that divination is only one of the possible uses for the cards. It may be that a different deck is—for you at least—best adapted to each separate purpose of the Tarot. Thus you might have one deck for divination, another for meditation, yet another for magical workings, and so on. Although some buy a large number of decks in an effort to find one that fits all situations, others collect Tarot decks just for the aesthetic appeal of the cards.

There may in fact be a deck that meets these qualifications for a given individual. In most

The Fool from Legend: The Arthurian Tarot

*Dukkerin' (Fortunetelling) from the
Buckland Gypsy Fortunetelling Deck*

cases, however, two or three decks will be required in order to obtain a proper and comfortable fit for the various uses to which the Tarot may be put by that person. A deck that is invaluable for divination may prove distracting or too abstract for pathworking. A deck used for magical workings may have too many associations to be useful in routine meditation. It is usually unrealistic to expect one deck to meet all possible needs. Of course, if you are only interested in one application, such as using the cards for divination only or for magic only, then one deck is quite sufficient. However, if you still have difficulty in choosing the one ideal deck for your purposes, then this book is for you.

"Approaching Vardo" from the
Buckland Gypsy Fortunetelling Deck

History of Tarot

There are many theories about the origin of the Tarot, but most of them are romances and fantasies—true in some corner of the astral plane, no doubt, but entirely unreal as far as mundane facts are concerned.

The facts as they are known are these: The first definite mention of playing cards in Europe is in a document from 1367 prohibiting their use in the canton of Bern, in what is now Switzerland. The first mention of cards that can be identified as Trumps was in the following century, and the earliest surviving Tarot cards are from that period; i.e., the mid-fifteenth century.

Many nineteenth-century writers stated that the Tarot cards must have been introduced into Europe by the Romany (Gypsies). They thought the Romany had originated in Egypt, hence the cards could be traced to the time of the Pharaohs. But the Romany did not arrive in

Europe until the beginning of the fourteenth century at the earliest, and the first unquestionable mention of them in the records dates to a hundred years later. The dating is very inexact, both as regards the cards and the Romany. Several modern authorities are of the opinion that the Romany arrived well after the cards, but the former opinion cannot be ruled out entirely. If so, however, the Romany brought the cards ultimately from India, not from Egypt as those authors supposed.

According to Paul Foster Case, founder of the Builders of the Adytum and author of *The Tarot: A Key to the Wisdom of the Ages* (1920), the Trumps were invented in Fez, Morrocco, in the twelfth century at a conference of the wise men of all religions. Presumably, he channeled this information. However, this idea is not too far from the assertion of Idries Shah (*The Sufis*, 1964) that the cards were devised as a Sufi teaching tool. In that case, they would most likely have originated in North Africa before appearing in Sicily and then in mainland Italy.

In any case, the idea that the cards originated in ancient Egypt (where cards were apparently unknown) seems to be entirely bogus. There is a regrettable tendency on the part of some organizations to seek legitimacy by tracing their lineage to ancient Egypt or to some other ancient culture, as if the Pharaoh Ankhenaton had sent his dues to some place in California every year. At one time, many Freemasons seriously believed that the fraternity originated, not in seventeenth-century England or even in the medieval guilds, but at the building of King Solomon's Temple. The same device is used to validate various ideas invented by occultist authors.

The first author to set forth the idea that the cards were of Egyptian origin was Court de Gebelin, in Paris in 1781. This idea was popularized by "Etteilla" (Alliette) a couple of years later. In 1856, Eliphas Lévi (Alphonse Louis Constant) popularized the idea that the 22 Trumps corresponded to the 22 letters of the Hebrew alphabet.

Before this time, no writer had ever made any mention of any esoteric or occult significance for the cards of the Tarot. In the exhaustive *De Occulta Philosophia* (1531), which examined every occult theory, every magical technique, and every divinatory method known at the time, Henry Cornelius Agrippa made no mention whatever of Tarot cards, or playing cards of any kind. At that time, the Tarot had been kicking around Europe for at least a century.

Nevertheless, it would be a mistake to say that the cards are just cards, good for nothing but playing games and designed for no other purpose. In the fourteenth and fifteenth centuries, there was no such thing as an entirely mundane artifact. What we now think of as "esoteric," "occult," or "mystical" ideas were part and parcel of society as a whole, not something separate, off to one side, to be attended to only by specialists or priests. Even in the High Renaissance, when Reason was beginning to gain its fatal foothold over Faith, it would have been unthinkable to produce a work of art, even so "low" an art as playing cards, for itself alone, with no allegorical meaning whatever. A card, like a pot or a trowel, had meaning beyond itself and was the mundane expression of something in higher realms. In this age of mass production, we have lost the spiritual significance of everyday objects; but when each item was individually crafted by a worker performing his *dharma* (that is, doing the thing he was born for and loved), matters were different. If the Fool is "nothing but" the village idiot, then it has to be remembered that the village idiot had a celestial and supernal correspondence all his own; he had significance beyond himself. He was a reflection of the macrocosm. For this reason, there can be no doubt that the Tarot has a traditional esoteric meaning, denatured and warped as it may have become in modern interpretations.

There is also the fact that the Tarot is what you make it. If you want it to be nothing but a mundane card game, then that is what it will remain, for you. If you want it to carry moral allegories and religious instruction, then it is admirably adapted to do just that. And if you see esoteric mysteries hidden therein, they will be there, for you.

One modern interpretation, or possibly one modern discovery, is that the 22 Trumps correspond to the 22 letters of the Hebrew alphabet. This may not be a simple coincidence. The qabalah, the elaborate and arcane system of Jewish mysticism and scriptural exegesis, was known by many educated men in Renaissance Italy where the cards first came to historical light, although it was not popularized until Pico della Mirandola did so in the latter part of the fifteenth century. Nevertheless, the number of Trumps was not necessarily settled before that time, so the correlation could indeed be intentional.

Be that as it may, the Trumps and the Hebrew alphabet were never mentioned in the same breath in public until Court de Gebelin noticed it, and it was left for Eliphas Lévi to work out the details in *Le Dogme et Rituel de la Haute Magie* (1856). Lévi's ideas were further popularized by Papus (Gerard Encausse) in *Le Tarot des Bohémiens* in 1889 and by Oswald Wirth, who published his Lévi-inspired designs for the Trumps in the same year. Both Papus and Wirth were members of H.P. Blavatsky's Theosophical Society.

So matters stood until the founding of the Hermetic Order of the Golden Dawn in London in 1887. Part of the inspiration for the foundation of the Order was a cipher manuscript either discovered or invented by W. Wynn Westcott, one of the Order's founders. The cipher proposed a new system of attributing the Hebrew letters to the Trumps that differed from Levi's system. As can be seen from the table on the opposite page, the Golden Dawn transposed the eighth and eleventh Trumps (Strength and Justice) in order to correlate more naturally with the order of the astrological signs, to which twelve letters (the

Correlation of Trumps and Hebrew Letters

Trump	Hebrew Letter	
	Lévi	Golden Dawn
Fool	Shin	Aleph
Magician	Aleph	Beth
High Priestess	Beth	Gimel
Empress	Gimel	Daleth
Emperor	Daleth	Heh
Hierophant	Heh	Vav
Lovers	Vav	Zayin
Chariot	Zayin	Cheth
Justice	Cheth	Lamed
Hermit	Teth	Yod
Wheel of Fortune	Yod	Kaph
Strength	Kaph	Teth
Hanged Man	Lamed	Mem
Death	Mem	Nun
Temperance	Nun	Samekh
Devil	Samekh	Ayin
Tower	Ayin	Peh
Star	Peh	Tzaddi
Moon	Tzaddi	Qoph
Sun	Qoph	Resh
Judgement	Resh	Shin
World	Tav	Tav

"single letters") of the Hebrew alphabet are attributed. It is very interesting, not to say instructive in the art of rhetoric, to read the respective justifications for the attributions— which are, of course, mutually contradictory.

The letters of the Hebrew alphabet are attributed to the twelve signs of the zodiac, the seven planets, and three of the four elements (Fire, Water, and Air). These attributions are of some importance in attributing the Tarot Trumps to the letters, because any such correlation also involves attributing the Trump to an astrological sign, a planet, or an element. It was for this reason that the Golden Dawn switched the order of Strength and Justice. Strength shows a lion and hence ought to go with Leo, whereas Justice, which includes the depiction of a pair of scales, logically goes with Libra.

Eliphas Lévi evidently did not have anything to say in print about the astrological attributions of the Hebrew letters, and Wirth considered only the zodiac (he attributed the other ten cards to other constellations). The Golden Dawn did make such attributions, however, as does the *Sepher Yetzirah*, the oldest qabalistic text, which dates back perhaps as early as the third century. The specific attributions were not part of the original *Sepher Yetzirah*, only the fact

Attributions of Hebrew letters

Hebrew Letter	Golden Dawn	*Sepher Yetzirah*
Aleph	Air	Air
Beth	Mercury	Saturn
Gimel	Moon	Jupiter
Daleth	Venus	Mars
Heh	Aries	Aries
Vav	Taurus	Taurus
Zayin	Gemini	Gemini
Cheth	Cancer	Cancer
Teth	Leo	Leo
Yod	Virgo	Virgo
Kaph	Jupiter	Sun
Lamed	Libra	Libra
Mem	Water	Water
Nun	Scorpio	Scorpio
Samekh	Sagittarius	Sagittarius
Ayin	Capricorn	Capricorn
Peh	Mars	Venus
Tzaddi	Aquarius	Aquarius
Qoph	Pisces	Pisces
Resh	Sun	Mercury
Shin	Fire	Fire
Tav	Saturn	Moon

that such an attribution could be made. Later addenda published with the text got down to specifics, however, and clearly spelled out which letter went with each sign and planet.

There are several versions of these addenda, but none of them correspond with the Golden Dawn system when it comes to the attribution of the seven "double letters" to the seven planets. The Order followed Etteilla in the attribution of the High Priestess to the Moon and the Empress to Venus, but differed otherwise. Why the Golden Dawn chose to deviate from the *Sepher Yetzirah* remains a matter of speculation. According to "true believers" in the Golden Dawn system, the attributions of both Lévi and the *Sepher Yetzirah* are "blinded"—intentionally misrepresented in order to hide the true secrets from the uninitiated. Modern Golden Dawn authorities, people who actually operate temples of the Order, no longer make this claim. After all, if information has to be "blinded" in order to be kept secret, why publish it at all?

Aleister Crowley, at one time a member of the Golden Dawn, introduced a further variation by transposing the Hebrew-letter attributions for the Emperor and the Star (Tzaddi and Heh, respectively). He did so because *The Book*

The Empress from the New Golden Dawn Ritual Tarot

The Emperor from the Rider/Waite deck

of the Law, which he channeled in Cairo in 1904, says, "All these old letters of my Book are aright; but צ [tzaddi] is not the Star." Crowley therefore interchanged Tzaddi with Heh in order to be symmetrical with the interchange of Teth and Lamed made earlier by the Golden Dawn. He seems to have remained confused about the astrological attributions of these two Trumps, however. To be truly consistent and symmetrical, the Emperor would have to be Aquarius and the Star would have to be Aries; yet these attributions seem disharmonious with the depictions on the cards.

The Golden Dawn version of the cards was never published before the 1970s, and even then it was not necessarily 100 percent correct until published by Sandra Tabatha Cicero and Chic Cicero in 1991. Prior to that time, members drew or painted their own decks according to the instructions of the Order. But in 1910, A.E. Waite published the first modern version of the Tarot that reflected any overtly esoteric interpretation. Although Waite was a member of the Golden Dawn, the Rider/Waite deck varies quite a bit from the official Golden Dawn version. This is at least partly because Waite felt himself still bound by the Order's oaths of secrecy. In fact, the "correct" (Golden Dawn) attributions of the Trumps to the Hebrew letters was not published until 1912, and then only in a small article in *The Occult Review.*

The Waite deck was the standard for many years simply because it was the only deck that was easily available in the United States. Paul Foster Case published a black-and-white version drawn by Jessie Burns Parke around 1930. His deck, designed for his order, the Builders of the Adytum—and hence known as the BOTA deck—is very similar to the Rider/Waite deck, but there are important differences. Finally, during the "occult revival" of the 1970s (which, oddly enough, coincided with the "Tolkien revival"), the Thoth deck of Aleister Crowley was published by Llewellyn Publications. At the same time, other decks began to appear, including a new edition of the Tarot of Marseilles by B. P. Grimaud of Paris. (Grimaud had first published this deck in 1930.) One of the first new decks to be published was the Aquarian Tarot designed by David Palladini (Morgan Press, 1970), and a traditional deck with French titles was published by U.S. Games of New York and A.G. Müller Cie. of Switzerland in the same year. This French deck was designated simply

Strength, from the Tarot 1JJ Deck

Justice, from the Aquarian Tarot

"Tarot Cards" and was specified as the "Tarot 1JJ Deck."

After that, the dam seemed to burst as a deluge of Tarot decks of hundreds of different designs began to flood the market in ever-increasing profusion and confusion. Stuart Kaplan has collected samples of many decks and published them in three volumes of *The Encyclopedia of Tarot* (U.S. Games, 1978, 1986, and 1990). U.S. Games (in Stamford, Connecticut) is currently the foremost publisher of Tarot decks as far as sheer quantity is concerned. The aspirant or student wading through this plethora of Tarot decks may well wonder which one to choose. That is what the rest of this book is about.

O

THE FOOL.

The Fool from the Rider/Waite deck

❧ 3 ❧

Divination by Tarot

By far the most popular and widespread use of the Tarot is as a tool for divination or fortune-telling. The Tarot is usually thought of as a for-tunetelling device. As such, the technical term applied to it is cartomancy, fortunetelling by cards. It therefore falls into the same class as palmistry, tea leaves, astrology, geomancy, crystal balls, and the random flight of birds.

Ordinary playing cards can also be used for divination, and still are, although this practice is not so widespread as it once was. One reason for its decrease in popularity is that Tarot decks have become so widely available that they have replaced ordinary playing cards as a means of divination. It is much easier to learn divinatory meanings for the picture cards of the Tarot than for the numbered cards of a poker deck.

In the earliest written reports that mention the Tarot, they are referred to as a device for fortunetelling and gambling. That means that they were used just the same way that regular playing cards are used today.

Ray Buckland's Gypsy Fortunetelling Deck represents a transitional stage between the older sets of playing cards with trumps and the modern esoteric cards used mainly for divination and not at all for card games. The numbered cards are the same as any modern pack of playing cards, and the face cards—depicting Romany individuals—include only king, queen, and jack. In addition, there are 22 trumps, the cards of the Boro Lil ("Big Book," or Major Arcana). These bear titles such as "Encampment," "Fortunetelling," and "Wise Woman" and hence do not correspond with the 22 traditional trumps now in use.

In many respects, the Buckland deck, so far from being a modern innovation, is a more traditional fortunetelling device than most modern Tarot decks based on nineteenth-century esoteric mystical interpretations. In addition, it has one advantage that other Tarot decks lack: if you learn the meanings of the numbered cards, you will be able to practice divination with any deck of cards, whether it has pictures on all the cards or not, including a standard deck of cards used for bridge or poker. The

"Pulling" from the Buckland Gypsy Fortunetelling Deck

"The Seeker" from the Buckland Gypsy Fortunetelling Deck

beginner, however, may prefer to start out with a deck that has the meanings of all the cards either depicted or written out in so many words on the cards themselves.

If you would rather avoid the esoteric decks and wish to learn the meanings of the minor cards of a standard deck of playing cards without having to consult a book in every instance, you could buy a cheap deck of bridge cards and write the meanings directly on the cards. Then, when these have been learned through continued use or by using the flash-card approach, this practice deck can be discarded.

Telling fortunes by means of the Tarot has become quite an industry, and there are hundreds, perhaps thousands, of commercial "readers" of various levels of competence. Many of them will do it over the phone for you if you dial their 900 number. There are also computer programs that will shuffle, deal, and interpret the cards for you. But by far the cheapest and easiest—and best—method is to learn how to read the cards yourself.

In the beginning, that will mean dealing the cards into a pre-set pattern, or spread, and looking up the meaning of each card in some book. I and thousands of other people in the late

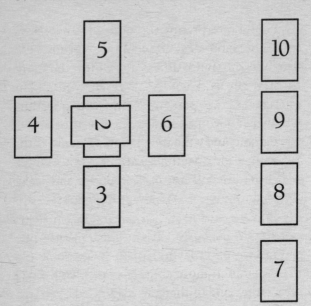

*Ancient Celtic Method of Divination
as developed by A.E. Waite*

1960s and early 1970s did just this with Eden Gray's still invaluable book, *The Tarot Revealed* (Signet, 1960), which used the Rider/Waite deck. We were also casting charts with Joseph F. Goodavage's *Write Your Own Horoscope* (Signet, 1968).

There will come a time, though, when you will get a feel for the cards and no longer find it necessary or even helpful to look up the meanings in a book.

Before interpreting the cards, it is necessary to shuffle and deal them into a layout. The usual recommendation is to shuffle the cards three times and let the "querent" cut. (The querent is the person asking the question, whether it is you or somebody else.)

Far and away the most popular layout is the "Ancient Celtic Method of Divination," which is neither ancient nor Celtic but which is relatively simple without being too simple. It was presented by A.E. Waite in his book, *The Pictorial Key to the Tarot* (Rider, 1910). Waite presented two other layouts in the same book, but they are much more complicated. I have never seen either one of them actually used.

In order to use the "Ancient Celtic Method," you must first choose a "Significator" to represent the querent. The Significator is always a court card, since the court cards generally represent people. Waite gave a method for doing this based on age, hair color, and eye color. Another method of picking the Significator is to go by the Golden Dawn astrological correlations along with the querent's sun sign (for example, the Knight of Pentacles rules from 21° Leo to 20° Virgo). A method that is probably superior to both of these, however, is to let the querent select his or her own Significator from among the court cards. Whichever card "feels like you" is the one you should be using.

To summarize Waite's method, however:

Male younger than 40   King
Male older than 40   Knight
Female younger than 40   Page
Female older than 40   Queen

Waite says the following physical characteristics, which he recommends, may have to be disregarded in the case of obvious temperaments such as energetic or lethargic.

Significator Suit Characteristics			
Suit	Complexion	Hair	Eyes
Wands	Fair	Yellow or auburn	Blue
Cups	—	Light brown or dull fair	Gray or blue
Swords	Dull	Dark brown or gray	Hazel
Pentacles	Sallow or swarthy	Very dark brown or black	Dark

Once the Significator has been chosen, it is placed face up in a central position. Then take the next card and lay it face up on top of the Significator and say, "This covers him." (That's what Waite says, anyway. Naturally, in many instances you will want to say, "This covers her.") It is not clear to me why it is necessary to say anything, except to remind yourself or give a hint to the querent as to what this particular card is supposed to signify.

"This card," says Waite, "gives the influence which is affecting the person or matter of inquiry generally, the atmosphere of it in which the other currents work." As usual, Waite's florid prose tends to obscure what should be a very simple matter. Just call this card "general influences." Ideally, the card should show what the question is about (Pentacles = finance, Cups = love, etc.), but that cannot be depended upon. Crowley advises you to abandon the reading if this card, or a similar card in a different layout, does not reflect the nature of the inquiry, but I think that may be carrying things a bit too far. After all, what suit should turn up if it is a question about spiritual development by engaging in strife in order to secure money for a loved one?

In the Celtic method, you must also pay attention as to whether the card is in an upright position or if it is "reversed"; that is, upside down. (The only way it could be actually "reversed" is to be dealt face down, but that is the word Waite used, and it has been the standard terminology ever since.) Reversed cards have different meanings, usually negative.

The second card is laid across the first at right angles while saying, "This crosses him/her." This card shows "the nature of the obstacles in the matter."

The third card goes above the Significator: "This crowns him/her." Waite waffles on this one, for he says, "It represents (a) the querent's aim or ideal in the matter; (b) the best that can be achieved under the circumstances, but that which has not yet been made actual." Either what you want or the best you can get.

The fourth card goes beneath the Significator, and you say, "This is beneath him/her." Waite says, "It shews the foundation or basis of the matter, that which has already passed into actuality and which the Significator has made his own." This strikes me as somewhat peculiar wording. Shouldn't it be "which the Querent has made his/her own"? The Significator is just a card.

There may be a tendency to confuse the fourth card, which is "the foundation or basis of the matter," with the first card, which "gives the influence which is affecting the person or matter of inquiry generally." But the first card is "general influences," whereas the fourth card represents the circumstances that brought about the present situation and/or things that have already been accomplished toward the goal. Maybe instead of saying, "This is beneath him/her," it would be more helpful if you were to say, "This is done."

The fifth card goes behind the Significator (depending on which way he/she is looking in the picture on the card). Say, "This is behind him/her." This card "gives the influence that is just passed, or is now passing away."

The sixth card is placed in front of the Significator, and you say, "This is before him/her." "It shews the influence that is coming into action and will operate in the near future."

The cards will now form a cross, with cards on all four sides of the Significator as well as two cards on top of it, one of them crossing the other two. Now you will deal cards to the right of this cross, beginning with the card at the bottom of the new column.

The seventh card, on the bottom of the column, represents the querent or the question itself "and shews its position or attitude in the circumstances." It is not clear how the question itself can have an attitude, but this is more of Waite's obscure self-expression. The card is almost always taken to represent the querent. The eighth card, above the seventh, is the "house," which is to say "his environment and the tendencies at work therein which have an effect on the matter—for instance, his position in life, the influence of immediate friends, and so forth."

"The ninth card," says Waite, "gives his hopes or fears in the matter." Again, here is an opportunity for confusion, for the third card can represent "the Querent's aim or ideal in the matter." Surely "hopes or fears" is very, very close to being the same thing as "aim or ideal." The only difference I can see, really, is that "aim or ideal" is a little more definite. You may "hope" for happiness but "aim" at the resolution of a problem in a particular way.

The tenth and last card, at the top of the right-hand column, is "what will come, the final result, the culmination which is brought about by the influences shewn by the other cards that have been turned up in the divination." In other words, the final result. To summarize and simplify slightly:

1. General influences
2. Obstacles, negative influences
3. Goal, or the best that can be achieved
4. Background, foundation
5. Past influences (recent)
6. Future influences (soon)
7. Querent
8. Environment
9. Hopes or fears
10. Final result

In order to make this method a little more understandable, the following example reading is provided.

Query: "What will happen to the splinter group from my lodge?"

The querent looked through the court cards and selected the Knight of Pentacles to represent himself. The following results were then obtained:

1. Two of Pentacles
2. Six of Pentacles
3. Page of Pentacles
4. Seven of Cups
5. Eight of Cups reversed

  6. The Fool
  7. Two of Swords reversed
  8. Nine of Cups reversed
  9. Seven of Wands
  10. Eight of Wands

Using various interpretations of the cards from several authorities, the results can be outlined this way:

  1. Balance, harmony
  2. Generosity, philanthropy
  3. Respect for learning and new ideas
  4. Castles in the air
  5. Feasting, abandonment of the spiritual
  6. Folly; or, an important choice
  7. Release; beware of rogues
  8. Overindulgence
  9. Valor, strife
  10. Swiftness, approaching resolution

Of course none of the cards can be interpreted in isolation; everything else has to be taken into account and interwoven. Nevertheless, a superficial reading of the foregoing

EL ANGEL CUSTODIO

THE GUARDIAN ANGEL

O ANJO CUSTÓDIO

The Guardian Angel from the Tarot of the Orishas

spread might be this: Although the lodge was formerly in harmony, the desire to spread the benefits of the fraternity (by recruiting new members) led to disagreements. The goal of the dissidents was to instill the candidates with a respect for the intellectual, symbolic, and metaphysical side of the organization. They became ambitious in this direction and worked to achieve a dream that turned out to be unrealistic under the circumstances (perhaps to revive the whole organization as an authentic initiatory society).

The actual split was brought about by the materialistic orientation of some of the members, who placed very little value on esoteric instruction. Each faction will persist in its folly (as seen by the other faction), and each member must make an important choice as to which group he will follow: the mystics or the mundanes. The querent has made his choice and hence feels a sense of relief, but he must be careful of lodge brothers who would deceive him for their own ends. Meanwhile, the querent is probably worrying too much about the whole affair ("overindulgence"). He fears continued strife, but a final resolution is near. The cards do not indicate whether this resolution will be reconciliation or the formation of a new lodge; only that the conflict will be resolved.

Aside from ordinary "fortunetelling," the Tarot can also be used to answer questions relating to personal destiny or directions for spiritual growth. For this purpose, you might want to choose a deck that has special spiritual significance as far as you are concerned. One example of a spiritually oriented deck that might be chosen for this purpose is the Tarot of the Orishas, designed by Zolrak and painted by Dürkön, and based on the African religion Candomblé. What follows is a simple example of such a reading using Zolrak's Ansate Cross layout.

The Ansate Cross layout is shown on the next page. The meaning of the various positions is as follows:

1. The beginning or starting point
2. The wait (the time it takes to consider a specific matter, what happens in the course of time)
3. The present (now, at the time of consultation)
4. The future (what is going to happen, what will come)

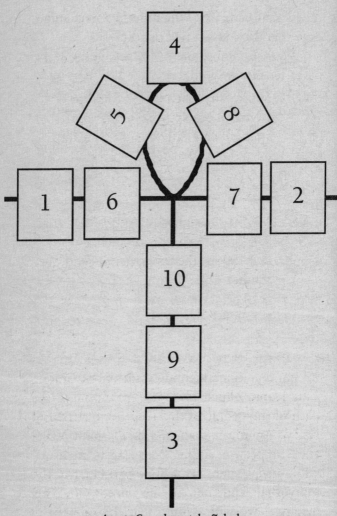

Ansate Cross layout, by Zolrak

5. Instinct (the function of instinct and feelings)

6. Accomplishment (that which becomes concrete)

7. Spirituality (the influence and/or advice of our spiritual guides, our strength and faith; what is true and devoid of any material interests)

8. Mentality (the collective unconscious, what we think and reflect upon)

9. Change (what transmutes or that which we must change)

10. Resolution (the last stage, the end, the results)

Query: "What path should I follow for spiritual development?"

When asking this question, the querent has in mind a dilemma not uncommon among Americans: which is more appropriate—the path of the people of this land (that is, that of Native American shamans) or the path of the ancestors (for example, European or African). Of course, the answer will be particular to the individual and her or his needs. In this instance, we will assume that the querent is male and has an African ancestry, although his forebears have been in this country for at least four generations.

The cards must be shuffled ten times for this layout. Having done so, we obtain the following result in this instance:

1. V of Fire, upside-down
2. Ogun
3. Message from Earth, upside-down
4. VII of Earth
5. Yemanya
6. The Earth
7. VII of Air
8. X of Water, upside-down
9. VI of Earth, upside-down
10. Dwarves and Gnomes, upside-down

Notice that Zolrak uses the term "upside-down" (*invertida*), a more accurate term than "reversed."

The meanings of the cards in any Tarot deck are multilayered and complex. It is misleading to attach one single restricted meaning to any one card or to give a capsule definition for it. This is particularly true with the Tarot of the Orishas, which is exceptionally deep and rich in symbolic meaning. Nevertheless, in an attempt to simplify this presentation, the following abbreviated meanings may be considered applicable in this particular reading:

1. End of struggle or dispute
2. Spirit triumphs over matter
3. Unwillingness to learn
4. Harvesting and checking
5. Woman or mother
6. Opening doors or paths
7. Confusion, lack of resources
8. Dead end after fruitless effort
9. Stubbornness; danger of bad contract
10. Selfish, materialistic attitude

The querent wishes to end his inner struggle and endless mental turmoil. Consequently, he has tentatively settled upon a path, but the conclusion cannot be final until he has recognized the fact that spirit must prevail over material concerns. At the present time, he is unwilling to listen to any further arguments and is not open to any new information. His mind is made up (yet he must have some doubts, or he would not be consulting the cards). He must now examine the results of his decision and compare them to his expectations and hopes. To do this, and in making a truly final decision, he must recognize his own feminine side and use this intuition. He has already examined many alternative paths that have been available to him, yet his lack of a true spiritual foundation has resulted in his confusion. He feels that all of his study and effort has been in vain; he is no more sure of his decision now than he was before he attempted to make one. He is in danger of making the wrong choice, so he should be less stubborn about coming to a decision on his own terms. If he is not cautious, his materialism and selfishness will cause him to choose a path for the wrong reasons.

You will notice that the cards did not address the implied question by indicating that he should choose one path or the other. Instead, they warned and admonished the querent in regard to his motives and methods. Before choosing a spiritual path, he must become unselfish and less materialistic, less concerned about what he will get out of his chosen path in the mundane details of his life.

There are many other divination layouts that have appeared in various books. Waite himself also presents layouts involving 42 and 35 cards. The Golden Dawn taught an extremely elaborate method involving five separate operations accompanied by ceremonial procedures. Eden Gray presented a Tree of Life method with ten cards, and Zolrak has several original layouts—two of them based on chakras and on the pyramids at Gizeh—in *The Tarot of the Orishas*. Donald Michael Kraig presents a rather more simple hexagram layout involving only the trumps in *Modern Magick*. The choice of layouts is yours.

So is the choice of a deck to use for divination, but there are several criteria that ought to be kept in mind when making such a choice.

If you intend to refer to the divinatory meanings in a book, or in several books, for your entire career as a reader of Tarot, then just about any old deck will do. You won't be looking at the images on the cards; you'll be looking at a book.

If, however, you wish to reach a point where you do not have to rely on a book—and every book has its limitations—then you will want to choose a deck whose images suggest possible divinatory interpretations. You cannot go by rote and book definitions in reading Tarot. The books are merely intended to be helpful and suggestive.

The true meanings of the cards in any given reading must be determined by you using both your knowledge gained from the books and your intuition. The result may end up being at variance with the standard book interpretation. For example, in the sample reading given above, the Two of Pentacles shows harmony and balance, but it also indicates that the balance is achieved only with effort and that the slightest mistake will result in disaster. This is shown clearly enough in the image on the Rider/Waite card, but you might miss that aspect of it if you go entirely by the book.

In the same reading, the Fool—perhaps the most important card in the reading, inasmuch as it is the only Trump—might be better interpreted as meaning that the querent is on the brink of a dangerous but significant turning point in his life; in that case, "folly" doesn't even enter into it. But the interpretation of an "important choice" appears in only one of several books; it is not a common reading for this card.

Because of the need for the cards to suggest interpretative ideas to your mind, even to your subconscious mind, and thus determining the overall tone or slant of the reading, the deck you choose for divination should probably follow the Rider/Waite tradition of using pictures on the numbered cards rather than simply having, for example, eight swords shown on the Eight of Swords.

The Crowley Thoth deck follows the older tradition of having the appropriate number of objects on each card of the Minor Arcana, rather than a scene of some kind, but it attempts to show the meaning of the card by the way in which the objects are drawn. As an added help in interpreting these cards, a key word (taken from the Golden Dawn papers) appears at the bottom of each card. For example, the Seven of Cups shows seven cups dripping a viscous, yellow-green liquid like mucous; the cups are catching the slime from poisonous-looking lotus flowers. At the bottom, the card is entitled "Debauch." The drawing succeeds in creating the impression of overabundance carried to the point of disgust, and we are further reminded of its nature by the astrological glyphs for Venus and Scorpio.

For this reason, you may prefer the Crowley deck for your divination efforts, especially if you have leanings toward Thelema and the teachings of the Great Beast. Speaking for myself, however, I really feel that the good old Rider/Waite deck, or some close modern variation of it, is ideal for the purpose of divination. I may be prejudiced in this regard, because the Rider/Waite was the deck I learned with over a period of years—during which it was the only deck available—and I had very good results with it right from the beginning. The graphic and suggestive images on the cards of the Minor Arcana along with the detail of the pictures of the Major Arcana make the Rider/Waite a good choice for purposes of divination.

I give second place to the Robin Wood Tarot, which is very similar to the Rider/Waite but which is rendered with much greater artistic ability. The images are actually much more evocative. The only reason I do not put it in first place is because of its Pagan/Wiccan orientation; for example, the Magician is shown with the antlers of a deer. This orientation may be enough to make it the deck of choice for many people of the Old Religion, but I personally tend to favor a Hermetic or Rosicrucian slant. Even so, I would be more inclined to accept the Robin Wood as the premier deck if it did not deviate in several important instances from the esoteric Rider/Waite (and BOTA) depictions, such as in the image shown on the Wheel of Fortune card. In the Robin Wood card, there is no sphinx or serpent and no depiction of Hermanubis; there is merely a drawing of a young woman experiencing various moods: joy at the top of the (roulette?) wheel and despair at the bottom. There is no angel or Cupid in the Lovers card and no devil in the Devil card.*

This is fine and quite valid if you are not particularly attracted to the mysteries of Hermetism or qabalah, but I am.

Notwithstanding all I have just said, however, I have to admit that the Robin Wood deck far outshines the Rider/Waite in the Minor Arcana. The images are basically the same, but they are rendered much more competently and much more evocatively.

There are a number of books that are useful for learning the basic divinatory meanings of the cards. Besides those already mentioned, I would recommend *How to Read the Tarot,* by Sylvia Abraham (Llewellyn, 1994) and *Tarot for Beginners,* by P. Scott Hollander (Llewellyn, 1995). And, of course, you will also want to consult the book, if any, that is intended to accompany your chosen deck.

The following examples of spreads are taken from a variety of sources.

---

* This might be interpreted as denying the reality of anything spiritual or nonmaterial, but I think the real intent is specifically to deny the reality of Judaeo-Christian angelology and demonology and their repressive, guilt-fostering implications.

Wheel of Fortune from Robin Wood Deck

Wheel of Fortune from the Rider/Waite Deck

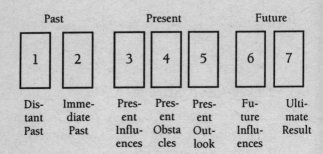

| Past | | Present | | | Future | |

Past		Present			Future	
1	2	3	4	5	6	7
Distant Past	Immediate Past	Present Influences	Present Obstacles	Present Outlook	Future Influences	Ultimate Result

The Seven-Card Spread

This spread is usually used for yes or no questions, according to A.E. Waite. If four or more cards are reversed then the answer is usually no, or little likelihood of a yes, or a delayed yes. The diviner may stop at this point, with the simple yes or no, or continue and read the symbolism of each card for a more complete picture.

The querent shuffles the cards asking the question aloud. The diviner then deals out the top seven cards from left to right.

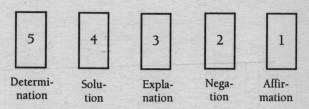

5	4	3	2	1
Determi-nation	Solu-tion	Expla-nation	Nega-tion	Affir-mation

The Five-Card Spread

This simple spread uses only the 22 Major Arcana cards. The Minor Arcana are removed from the deck. A Significator is necessary only if the question is about someone else. If this is the case, take the card from the Minor Arcana. Cards are shuffled by the reader. Cards are laid from right to left under the Significator. The querent is asked to pick a number from one to 22. The reader counts out that number and takes the last card. This is card number one. This process is continued, from one to 21, from one to 20, etc., until the five cards are drawn. Shuffle the deck each time.

Card One: Affirmation. This is what is going to happen. Card Two: Negation. This is what can or will prevent it from happening. Card Three: Discussion or Explanation. This is why you're in this situation. Card Four: Solution. This is what you can do about it, to either encourage or change it. Card Five: Determination. Depending on what steps you take, this is what will happen.

Seventeen-Card Spread

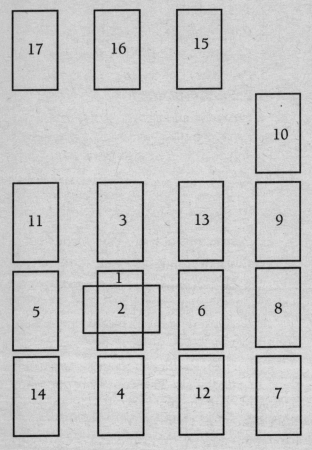

1. Querent's concern
2. The conflict
3. Happiness or sadness
4. Conditions of health or security
5. Past actions affecting the first card
6. Immediate future
7. Character and ego traits of querent
8. Outside influences affecting money and environment
9. Hopes and fears relating to the tenth card
10. Outcome
11. Past actions of family and friends
12. Illusions regarding question or secret enemies
13. Future plans
14. Past emotional concerns
15. 16. 17. Goals for the future.

The querent shuffles all the cards and hands them to the diviner. Start to lay out the cards beginning with the first place. All the cards are placed face up. Hold the deck in your right hand, pull the top card to you and over, repeating this action until all seventeen cards are placed in their right position and in order.

Check for court cards that will represent the people in the querent's life. Also look for predominant suits. These help you understand the question and the spread.

The Tree of Life Spread

The Tree of Life spread uses either all the cards or just the Major Arcana cards. Try it both ways and see which you prefer. After the cards are shuffled and returned to you, begin laying them out starting from number ten and ending on number one. Every sphere has its own explanation. These examples should give you an idea of how to read this spread. The Tree of Life spread covers many areas and has the potential to answer any or all questions.

1.
LIGHT

Outcome

3.
UNDER-
STAND-

Receptivity,
Limitations,
Creativity

2.
WISDOM

Power, Goals,
Changes

5.
SEVER-
ITY

Activity,
Destruction,
Struggle

6.
BEAUTY

New insights,
Compassion,
Love

4.
MERCY

Memories,
Abundance,
Generosity

8.
GLORY

Discrimination,
Analysis,
Knowledge

9.
FOUNDA-
TION

Subconscious
fears, Illusions,
Sexual focus

7.
VICTORY

Desires,
Emotions,
Romance

10.
KING-
DOM

Practicality,
Money, Physical
possession

The High Priestess from the Rider/Waite deck

❧ 4 ❧

Meditation with Tarot

To use the Tarot for divination only is to neglect its enormous potential as a tool for spiritual development. In fact, some say that it is a debasement of the purpose of the cards to use them for divination at all. A.E. Waite seemed to be of that opinion, referring to such divination as "vulgar fortune-telling." Ironically, Waite also popularized the so-called "Ancient Celtic Method of Divination" described in the last chapter and by far the most widely used method of divination today. As far as he was concerned, however, the use of the Tarot for divination was merely a "veil" concealing its true purpose, which is to convey a "secret doctrine, which is the realization by the few of truths imbedded in the consciousness of all, though they have not passed into express recognition by ordinary men."

The cards of the Major Arcana in particular embody, as Waite says, "symbolical presentations of universal ideas …"; that is, they represent what Jung called the archetypes of the collective unconscious.

The idea behind using the Tarot as a tool for meditation is that you can come into contact with these archetypes and use them to alter and improve your well-being—physical, emotional, psychological, and spiritual.

So how do you meditate with the cards? Several methods have been described by various authors. Whatever technique you use, however, you should begin by relaxing thoroughly, but in such a way that you are not likely to fall asleep.

The most effective approach is to sit in a comfortable position. Stretch out your arms and work your shoulders around to get out the worst of the kinks and tensions. Then close your eyes and concentrate on each part of your body in turn, telling it to relax. It may help to tense the muscles in the area and then suddenly let go and relax them.

Begin with your feet. You can mentally repeat some simple affirmation, such as, "My left foot is relaxed. I feel the tension draining from the muscles in my left foot. It is relaxing … relaxing … totally relaxed." Then go on to the left calf, the left knee, the left thigh, and so on until your whole left leg is totally relaxed. Then do the same with your right leg and go on to the abdomen, the lower back, the chest, the upper back, the shoulders, the arms (beginning with each hand and working toward the shoulder), the shoulders again, the neck and throat, the muscles of the face, the forehead, even the top of the head. I mention the shoulders twice because most people concentrate all their tension in the shoulders. It is important to get rid of that tension, or at least reduce it as much as possible. When you have gone over your whole body in this way, think to yourself, "I am now totally relaxed … totally relaxed."

After you have been doing this relaxation technique for quite some time, it should be possible to program yourself to achieve the same state, or something very similar to it, simply by closing your eyes and counting down from 10 to 1, or even, for the very advanced, from 3 to 1. Go on down to zero for a more profound state of relaxation.

Once you are in a relaxed state, you can begin your meditation.

In *Modern Magick*, Donald Michael Kraig describes a method of scanning a Tarot card—minutely examining the design from left to right in half-inch bands, a simplified version of the way a television image is created on the screen of a TV set. The same process is then followed in the imagination, with eyes closed. The complete image is then mentally erased in the same manner. Once the entire card has been erased, you will ideally go immediately into a state of pure consciousness without thought.

Like all techniques, this approach works better for some people than for others. You should experiment with various methods of meditation until you find one that you are comfortable with and that seems to work for you.

Another very useful method of Tarot meditation does not aim at achieving a state of no-thought, although that could easily be the result. In this method, taught by the Builders of the Adytum (BOTA), you simply stare at one of the Trumps for five minutes, noting all the details of the card and focusing your attention upon it. If you try this method, you will find that five minutes is not so long that you become bored or that your mind begins to wander. No results will be immediately apparent in most cases—you will almost certainly not experience anything similar to a meditative state while actually looking at the card—but later in the day you may well notice a difference in your

The Magician from Legend: The Arthurian Tarot

mental state or general outlook on life. You may even notice that things begin to go your way instead of seeming to rise up deliberately in order to frustrate you.

Another form of meditation with the cards is to look at a Trump, or even a card from the Minor Arcana, for less than a minute and then concentrate for twenty minutes or more on visualizing that card and holding the image in your mind's eye. Such concentration as this is not easy to attain, of course, although it is excellent training in visualization. You might want to become good at visualization for several reasons. It comes in very handy in meditation techniques because it enables you to concentrate on a visualized object. This object does not always have to be a Tarot card; it could be a simple object such as a candle flame. Of course, visualization is also a proven technique for achieving goals and getting what you want (see *The Llewellyn Practical Guide to Creative Visualization* by Denning and Phillips), and it comes in very handy in any sort of magic, whether ceremonial or shamanic.

Meditation by concentrating on the visualized image of a Tarot card comes closer to being true meditation, wherein a state of "no-

The Fool of the BOTA Deck

Death from the Healing Earth Tarot by David and Jyoti McKie

thought" is attained by concentration. In other practices not involving the Tarot, the concentration could be on an object, or on an internal event such as the breath or an external sound that is not disharmonious.

When you stare at a card, even if you are not yet ready to try visualization, you should pay attention to the details of the card. In the case of the BOTA Fool card, what images appear on his satchel? On his cloak? What does he have on his head? What is around his waist? By deliberately noticing such details as these, you will find it easier to visualize the card when you are ready to try that step. Not only that, but your subconscious mind will begin to absorb the inner meaning of the card and put its lessons to work in your life.

A more advanced form of this meditation is to imagine the Trump floating above your head with the central figure in the card being life-size. The image is then allowed to descend until you merge with the figure and become that person yourself. In the BOTA teachings, there are specific techniques and affirmations connected with this form of Tarot meditation, but I am not at liberty to give them here.

Simply concentrating on a specific card once a day, going through all 22 Trumps in

The Moon from Legend: The Arthurian Tarot

turn, will have a beneficial effect on your spiritual progress and your overall well-being. However, these meditations may also be directed toward specific purposes according to the significance of the Trump you are using. Some of the following descriptions might seem to apply to fairly mundane matters, and the cards are undoubtedly useful in that regard, but each card also has an esoteric beneficial effect on your total spiritual being. These effects are frequently difficult to put into words that mean anything, so I have not attempted to do so, but they are nevertheless quite real.

- The Fool—to overcome depression; to tap into cosmic consciousness
- The Magician—to improve attention and concentration
- The High Priestess—to improve the memory
- The Empress—to enhance your imaginative faculty
- The Emperor—to improve the reasoning faculty of the brain; to help you get organized and introduce order into your life and surroundings
- The Hierophant—to improve your

intuition; to enable or enhance your
ability to hear your own inner voice

- The Lovers—to enhance your ability to
  discriminate, to choose the better of
  two alternatives
- The Chariot—to help make you more
  receptive to the Higher Will
- Strength—to enhance the receptivity of
  your subconscious mind to suggestions
  from the higher mind or supercon-
  sciousness—or to the influence of the
  Tarot Trumps on your subconscious in
  these meditations
- The Hermit—to aid in your search for
  cosmic consciousness; to help you
  cope with being alone; to enhance your
  sense of touch; to help you remember
  dreams
- The Wheel of Fortune—to help you
  adapt to changing circumstances; to
  help you focus on your goals and
  objectives
- Justice—to bring about balance in your
  character or in your life; to enhance
  your ability to imagine and visualize a
  desired object

The Priestess from the New Golden Dawn Ritual Tarot

- The Hanged Man—to enhance your ability to adapt to new ways of thinking, new ways of seeing things
- Death—to bring about or adapt to transformation; to help you determine what you really want

The Chariot from the Witches Tarot

- Temperance—to help in meeting and passing any sort of test or trial; to help you determine the best way to achieve your desires
- The Devil—to dispel ignorance; to develop an improved sense of humor; to help you visualize logical outcomes
- The Tower—to help you see things as they are; to help you apply logical thinking to determining what you really want and to the process of attaining it
- The Star—to enhance your ability to meditate; to help you recognize your lower desires for what they are
- The Moon—to enhance your awareness of your body and its needs
- The Sun—to aid in healing—physical, mental, or spiritual; to overcome lower desires with reason
- Judgment—to help you make a decision; to aid you in deciding what is best for your body in the way of diet and exercise
- The World—to aid in concentration, to help you define a problem; to help you recognize what your body requires

Choosing the Right Deck

Choosing a deck for meditation should be fairly easy. Ordinarily, you would simply pick the deck that you were most comfortable looking at—one with pleasing images—and one that tended to put you in a receptive frame of mind. However, for meditation, and particularly for meditation on specific cards for specific purposes, the cards should be rich in symbolism that will speak directly to your unconscious mind. For this reason, most of the decks that are specific to some particular culture or system and that have little symbolic detail are not very good for meditation.

The Crowley Thoth deck is specific to a certain system—Thelema—but is nevertheless rich in detailed symbolism that is directly related to the archetypes. The Enochian Tarot, although in many respects not a true Tarot deck and featuring little detail, contains extremely evocative images that may be useful for those following this path. On the other hand, a deck such as the Witches Tarot, produced by Ellen Cannon Reed and Martin Cannon, although a valuable and interesting deck in many respects, is so stripped of esoteric details as to be of little use for deeper meditation—certainly for any meditation designed to alter the psyche with the object of achieving concrete results. Indeed, it is not designed for that purpose; its primary function is as a tool for divination.

My own personal recommendation for a Tarot deck with Trumps that are especially useful for meditation, having been designed with an unequaled richness of esoteric detail attractively portrayed, is the black-and-white BOTA deck, preferably hand-colored by the student. The BOTA deck was designed by Paul Foster Case and drawn by Jessie Burns Parke. Case himself felt that the result was a little too imitative of the Rider/Waite deck, but he did manage to correct much of Waite's symbolism. Waite deliberately made some of the symbols a bit obscure in order to hide the true meanings of the cards, which he may have felt bound by oath to conceal. Case, however, felt that this symbolic information should be available to all. The resulting symbolism, although it follows the basic ideas of the Golden Dawn, is rich indeed. It also has the advantage of being universal; it is not peculiar to any specific path or religion the way so many "theme" Tarot decks are; instead it incorporates universal archetypal images meaningful to everybody—or at least, to the subconscious mind of everybody.

39. NOOS

LESSER SEPHIROTHIC CROSS
ANGELS OF FIRE

NOOS, from the Enochian Tarot

It may well be that Paul Foster Case designed the BOTA deck specifically for meditation, for the Order's correspondence lessons devote a great deal of attention to this use of the cards. The cards sold by BOTA are not colored, but have black-and-white outlines. The student is supposed to do the coloring with colored pencils or watercolors, and this, too, constitutes a form of meditation because it forces you to concentrate on the details of the card.

Whatever deck you choose for this purpose, good luck to you in your meditations. May they help you to achieve the result you seek.

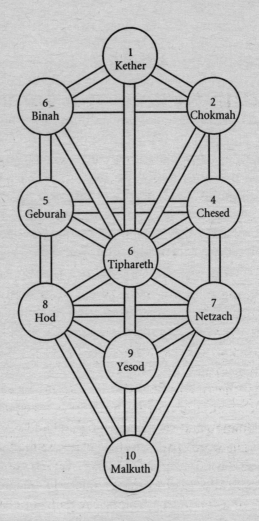

The Qabalistic Tree of Life

❦ 5 ❧

Pathworking with Tarot

Using the Tarot for pathworking is really a natural development or progression from using it for meditation. In both cases, you "go into your head" for some length of time set aside for the purpose. Meditation is the more passive of the two approaches, and it is strongly recommended that you do not try to undertake pathworking until you have practiced meditation techniques with the Tarot for a few months. There is really no particular danger involved for anyone with a stable personality, but the results will be pale and unimpressive compared to what they might be if you had devoted a suitable amount of time to the simpler practice of meditation and visualization beforehand.

The word "pathworking" is in common use these days, but it is not always very accurate. Specifically, "pathworking" refers to imaginative or astral journeys along the paths or channels of the symbolic qabalistic diagram known

as the Tree of Life, or Tree of the Sephiroth.
There are 22 of these paths, and each one corre-
sponds to a Hebrew letter and to a Tarot trump.
The theory is that the trumps can be used as
"doors" for entering the corresponding paths.

In recent years, however, the term "pathworking" has come to mean almost any imaginative journey. This is what the great Swiss
psychologist Carl Jung referred to as "active
imagination." If you actually leave your body
and make the journey by astral projection, there
is really not much difference in the results—
except that the out-of-body experience would be
more vivid and memorable.

At this point, it should probably be empha-
sized that it would be misleading if you were to
make the common error of confusing psychic
events with spiritual ones. If you meet a goddess during a pathworking or astral experience,
it could conceivably be a real goddess manifest-
ing on a lower plane, just as the Virgin frequently manifests to certain individuals on the
material plane. More than likely, however, it is
your own psychological construct. That does
not mean that it has no value, merely that the
manifestation should not be taken as in any
way transformative or extraordinary. You have

◗LLEWELLYN
New Worlds of Mind and Spirit

TAROT
Decks & Kits

Kit Box

Book

Layout Sheet

Deck

EGEND:
The Arthurian
Tarot Kit

he romantic, turbulent age of rthurian Britain comes alive in this reathtaking new Tarot. Along with raditional Tarot symbolism, these nages depict a compelling historial saga and a colorful cast of characters that evoke major archetypes f human psychology. These cards re easy to interpret because their neaning is expressed in the drama f the egend. The watercolor paintings re graceful ambassadors of the therworld, seducing the reader into the intuitive state needed for effective psychic interpretations. In keeping with the historical context of the Dark Ages, the fusion of both Pagan and Christian beliefs are embodied in the paintings. Accompanying the deck is a 22" x 25" Celtic Cross color layout sheet and the book *A Keeper of Words,* which lists the divinatory meanings of each card, the legend associated with it, and a description of the symbolism.

AVAILABLE MAY 1995 • 79 cards with 304-pg. book and layout sheet
reated & Illustrated by Anna-Marie Ferguson • Order #K-267-4 • $34.95

All Tarot Decks and Kits are available from your local bookstore
Or, call 1-800-THE-MOON to order direct from Llewellyn

Kit Box

Book

The Tarot of the Orishas Kit

Here, at last, is a Tarot that represents the magical thinking of ancient Africa. This remarkable new deck employs the powerful energies of the Candomblé religion of Brazil. Candomblé originated with the Yoruba people of west-central Africa and is similar to Santería in its worship of the Orishas. The 77 breathtaking cards, created by an initiate and priest of Candomblé, are based on numerology, astrology and other branches of metaphysics.

The 25 cards of the "Major Arcana" represent the Orishas. The remaining 52 "Minor Arcana" cards are divided into four groups of 13 cards each, representing the four elements. The accompanying book delves into the origins and symbolism of each card, which together provide lessons for your daily life that go beyond the material world, getting to the essence of all things: the Spirit.

77 cards in English, Spanish & Portuguese with 384-pg. book in English & Spanish • Created by Zolrak • Illustrated by Durkon
Order #K-842-7 • $29.95

ALSO SOLD SEPARATELY: *THE DECK: Order #K-843-5 • $19.95*
THE BOOK: Order #K-844-3 • $12.95

The Healing Earth Tarot Kit

Kit Box

Book

The Healing Earth Tarot Kit:
A Journey in Self Discovery,
Empowerment & Planetary Healing
is a shamanic Tarot that takes a
bold new approach for today's world
climate. It draws together teachings
from tribal wisdom across the
globe—including Aboriginal, African,
Celtic and Native American. The
Major Arcana reflects a new
spiritual consciousness: for
example "The Wise Old Woman"
replaces "The Hermit," "The
Shaman" replaces "The Magician,"
and "The Native American Medicine
Loop" replaces "The Wheel of
Fortune."

To the Minor Arcana are added two
new suits that acknowledge subtle
energies: "Feathers" (the psychic
realm & spirit) and "Pipes" (healing
& herbal lore). The traditional Court
Card imagery of European nobility is
replaced with "grandparents" from
cultures attuned to the sacredness
of all Earth life. Used with the
accompanying book, the cards may
be drawn individually for daily guidance or laid out in appropriate
spreads. Their clarity and beauty
enable you to access your own inner
knowing and ask for help with any
aspect of your life.

106 cards with 288-pg. book • Created & Illustrated by
Jyoti & David McKie • Order #K-454-5 • $34.95

The Witches Tarot Deck

The Witches Tarot Deck is the first Tarot to present the mystical Qabalistic symbolism from a pagan point of view. Qabalist and pagan Ellen Cannon Reed gives new interpretations to traditional Major Arcana symbolism. Meditate on the "The Horned One" in place of "The Devil," "The High Priest" in place of "The Hierophant," and "The Seeker" in place of "The Hermit." The Minor Arcana are depicted in a unique and newly symbolic fashion. Each of the Magical Spheres is included, in striping color, on the corresponding cards.

78 cards with instructions • Created by Ellen Cannon Reed
Illustrated by Martin Cannon • Order #L-669-7 • $19.95

The Witches Tarot (book) is the companion guide to the deck, describing how the symbols of the Tarot relate to the paths of the Qabalistic Tree of Life *and* to the Craft. It is said that the spheres represent the states of being, and the paths represent the states of becoming. Learn how to use this tarot on your spiritual journey. *Ellen Cannon Reed • 320 pg. • illus. • Order #L-668-9 • $9.95*
AVAILABLE IN KIT FOR OCT. 1995

The
ROBIN WOOD
TAROT

1 The Magician 1

1

19   19

The Sun

The High Priestess

2   2

The Robin Wood Tarot

The Robin Wood Tarot is a gift to your visual and psychic senses, and it is amazingly easy to understand and interpret. Loosely based on the images of the Rider-Waite deck, Robin Wood's interpretation is more current, natural and light. Anyone will enjoy using this deck, as the symbolism is not specific to any one belief system or tradition. The shining strength of this Tarot lies in its depiction of the Minor Arcana; the cards are richly illustrated with visual reminders of the most common meanings built into the figures. Key words in the instruction booklet serve as memory aids for cards the Ace through 10. Tap into the wisdom of your subconscious with one of the most beautiful Tarot decks on the market today!

78 cards with instructions
Created & illustrated by Robin Wood
Order #L-894-0 • $19.95

The Enochian Tarot Deck

71. XTMP

LESSER ANGELS OF WATER

78. AHMLLKV

SENIOR OF EARTH

THE ENOCHIAN TAROT

Gerald & Betty Schueler
Sallie Ann Glassman

17. TAN

THE BALANCE

The Enochian Tarot Deck is based upon the principles of Enochian Magick and was designed to be a medium of enlightenment. It is a map into the realms of spiritual bliss – a record of our relationship with the cosmos. Illustrated with vivid primordial images that incorporate a Crowleyan flavor, each card of the expanded Major Arcana represents one of the 30 regions of the magical universe and represents qualities such as Doubt, Intuition and Glory. The Minor Arcana contains 56 cards representing a deity, or group of deities, that inhabit the four Enochian Watchtowers. They are thought to be some of the most powerful angels you can contact. By using an appropriate ritual or meditation, a magician can use these cards to enter regions of the invisible worlds.

86 cards with instructions • Created by Gerald & Betty Schueler
Illustrated by Sallie Ann Glassman • Order #L-708-1 • $12.95

The Enochian Tarot (book) serves as a quick and handy reference to the use of the Enochian Tarot Deck for either divination or meditation. It contains a great deal of detailed information, including gematria, correspondences and magical formulas, but is written so anyone can use the deck immediately. *Gerald & Betty Schueler*
352 pg. • illus. • Order #L-709-X • $12.95
ALSO AVAILABLE IN KIT FOR OCT. 1995

The New Golden Dawn Ritual Tarot Deck

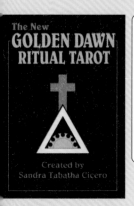

The New
GOLDEN DAWN
RITUAL TAROT

Created by
Sandra Tabatha Cicero

THE PRINCE OF CUPS

CUPS 1 CUPS

The Ace of Cups

8

STRENGTH

This Tarot was encouraged by Israel Regardie and painted entirely by an active Adept of the Hermetic Order of the Golden Dawn. It is the first of its kind to skillfully blend the descriptions given in the initiation ceremonies of the Golden Dawn with traditional Tarot imagery. The result is a visually stunning, sensual deck that is perfect for meditation, divination and ritual work. No other deck contains two versions of the Temperance card (as specified in Golden Dawn ritual), and no other deck makes interpretation so easy by presenting the corresponding Hebrew letter, planetary and zodiacal symbols for each card. Also featured are the Golden Dawn "flashing colors" and the Qabalistic color scales. This is a ritual deck for a lifetime.

79 cards with instructions • Created & illustrated by Sandra Tabatha Cicero • Order #L-138-5 • $19.95

The New Golden Dawn Ritual Tarot (book) is for both the newcomer and advanced magician. It contains enough material to give the beginner a basic understanding of Qabalah and Tarot fundamentals, while satisfying the skilled magician's need for powerful ritual work.

Chic Cicero & Sandra Tabatha Cicero • 256 pg. illus. • Order #L-139-3 • $14.95
ALSO AVAILABLE IN KIT FOR OCT. 1995

Buckland's Complete Gypsy Fortuneteller Kit contains everything you need to perform divination in the Gypsy tradition. **The Buckland Gypsy Fortunetelling Deck** is derived from the cards used by an authentic Gypsy family. The book *Secrets of Gypsy Fortunetelling* discusses the language, history and magical practices of the Gypsies. The Kit also includes a double-sided Gypsy layout sheet.
74 cards with instructions, 240-pg. book & 18" x 24" layout sheet
Created by Ray Buckland • Order #L-055-9 • $19.95

ALSO SOLD SEPARATELY: THE DECK: Order #L-052-4 • $12.95
THE BOOK: Secrets of Gypsy Fortunetelling: Order #L-051-6 • $4.99

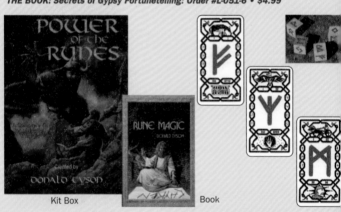

Kit Box   Book

Power of the Runes Kit is a complete Rune divination system. **The Rune Magic Deck** makes up the world's first rune deck and features a striking design that boldly portrays the 24 futhark runes. The book *Rune Magic* presents a system of runework that partakes of the essence of the ancient Teutonic tradition. All known information o the use of the runes is condensed in this readable and accessible format.
24 cards with instructions, 4 wooden Rune Dice, and 224-pg. book • Created by Donald Tyson • Cards illuminated by Robin Wood • Order #L-828-2 • $24.95
ALSO SOLD SEPARATELY: Rune Magic Deck: Order #L-827-4 • $12.95
                         Rune Magic (Book):   Order #L-826-6 • $10.95

Queen of Wands from the Robin Wood Tarot deck

not advanced a rung on the ladder of spiritual attainment. You have not been initiated into the Fellowship of Saints. You are under no obligations to spread the gospel of a new religion revealed to you alone. If you meet a departed loved one, it is not that person's spirit; it is your idea of that person, your remembrance of him or her. Nevertheless, you can learn something about yourself from the experience, and the first step on any spiritual path is to know yourself. The important thing to remember is that the astral plane, where these journeys take place, is rather low on the hierarchy of planes and is still very remote from anything actually spiritual.

On the other hand, the danger does exist that, if you are too self-indulgent or self-deluded on these journeys, you will be opening yet further rifts into the lower world of counterfeit spirituality and the forces of dissolution.

The method for pathworking, whether or not you associate the cards with their qabalistic correspondences, is really rather simple. The first step must be to perform some ritual of protection. If you do this, it will minimize the chance of interference by astral vagrants such as shells of the dead, demons, and miscellaneous astral detritus. If you are actually trying to work a specific path, it will help prevent you from straying from that path. If nothing else, it will center you and improve your concentration. It will also decrease the chances of delusion and deception and lessen the possibility that you will inadvertently open the gates to inferior forces.

There are many rituals of protection that can be used, and you may already have one that you favor. My own preference is for the Lesser Banishing Ritual of the Pentagram as taught by the Hermetic Order of the Golden Dawn a hundred years ago and still in general use among magicians, witches, and pagans of all persuasions. If you object to the Judaeo-Christian archangels or the Hebrew language, you can easily substitute any other language and the deities, demigods, or spiritual beings of any other tradition.

The pentagram ritual has been printed so many times in so many different places, that it seems almost a waste of time and space, as well as a trial on the patience of the reader, to repeat it here. Nevertheless, many readers of this book may never have heard of it and will not have any book that describes it.

Begin with the relaxation procedure described in the last chapter. Then stand up and face the east in the center of the room where you will carry out the pathworking. Close your eyes and imagine that you are becoming taller and larger. Soon you are looking down on the roof of the house and then on the receding landscape, as if you were riding a rocket to the moon. The earth is left behind, and you continue to grow faster than the speed of light, your head among the planets and then among the stars. Meanwhile, your feet remain rooted to the earth.

Then you will perceive a distant, tiny spark above your head that grows larger and larger as you approach in your growth. This is the divine light. (This will not necessarily happen automatically unless you have been practicing every day for a while. That is no problem, however; simply will it to happen; imagine that it is happening.) When the brilliant source of heavenly light, now the size of a basketball, is directly above your head, reach up and touch it with the forefinger of your right hand. Draw the light into your brain, where it illuminates the whole area behind your eyes and floods your head with light. At this point, you should say, in a vibrant, full voice, *"Ateh."* This is a Hebrew word meaning "Thine is." The exact pronunciation is not too important: it can be ah-teh or ah-tay or ah-tah; whichever suits you best.

Then move your finger to the middle of your chest, or lower down to your solar plexus. (Optionally, move your finger to the area of your groin. This may actually be more "accurate," but for many people it may awaken distracting sexual associations.) Visualize a shaft of shining white light moving down through your body and extending to infinity beneath your feet. Say *"Malkuth"* (mal-koot or mal-kooth—"mal" can rhyme with either "Al" or "all"). This is another Hebrew word meaning "kingdom." So far, you have said "Thine is the kingdom." Sound familiar?

Next, touch your right shoulder and say, *"Ve-Geburah"* (vay-ge-BOO-ra), which means "and the power." Visualize another shaft of white light extending from your heart area out your right shoulder to infinity.

Students of the *Zohar*, the medieval qabalistic text, may object at this point because, in the original tradition, the Sephirah Geburah is definitely on the left side of the body, while Chesed (or Gedullah) is on the right. Several generations of practitioners and would-be magicians have been ignoring the *Zohar*, however—it isn't readily available, after all—and associating Geburah with the right shoulder. You should use whichever method you feel most comfortable with. If you wish to adhere to the formulation of the *Zohar*, simply touch your *left* shoulder when you say "Geburah," and imagine the shaft of light extending out your left shoulder.

To complete the cross, touch your left (or right) shoulder and say *"Ve-Gedullah"* (vay-ge-DOO-la), which means "and the glory." Visualize the horizontal shaft of light now extending from your heart area out your left shoulder to infinity. You are now impaled on a cross of light.

Finally, clasp your hands in front of your chest and say, *"Le-olahm. Amen"* (leh-o-LAM. Ah-men)—"Forever and ever. Amen." Vividly imagine the cross centering and energizing your whole being.

Then go to the east side of the room, or simply continue to face east. Using your forefinger (or a stick of incense, or a wand, or a dagger), trace a large pentagram in the air in front of you, extending from your hips to a point above your head. Start at the lower left corner. Visualize the pentagram actually appearing before you in brilliant blue-white light as you trace it. Authoritatively point your finger at the center of the pentagram and say, in a loud and vibrating voice that penetrates to the farthest corner of the Universe, *"Yod-Hay-Vav-*

Hay." This is the Tetragrammaton, the four-lettered name of God.

Some people prefer to use a Golden Dawn gesture referred to as "The Sign of the Enterer" when vibrating this and the other God names of the pentagram ritual. You may do this if you wish. The gesture involves lunging forward on your left foot and shooting your arms out to full length from a position with your hands next to your ears. Mickey Mouse uses the Sign of the Enterer frequently in the "Sorcerer's Apprentice" sequence of the Walt Disney movie, *Fantasia.*

Move around to the south, or face the south, using your finger or implement to trace a line from the center of the pentagram to a corresponding point in the south. Repeat the pentagram and the gesture, this time vibrating *"Adonai"* (add-oh-nye). Then repeat in the west with *"Eheieh"* (eh-heh-yeh) and the north with *"Agla"* (ah-ge-lah). Then return to the east. When you make the circuit with the pentagrams, continue to trace the line from one pentagram to the next until you have made a closed circle of shimmering blue-white light connecting the four pentagrams from center to center.

Then return to the center, your starting point, and extend your arms out to the sides.

Say, "Before me, Raphael. Behind me, Gabriel. At my right hand, Michael. At my left hand, Auriel. Before me flames the pentagram; behind me shines the six-rayed star."

The names are the names of the four chief archangels and should be "vibrated" (spoken audibly in an authoritative, vibrant voice that you visualize as penetrating into, vibrating, and energizing the entire cosmos). You should also visualize the archangels, bearing in mind that Raphael is the archangel of Air, Michael of Fire, Gabriel of Water, and Auriel of Earth. According to some authorities, they should be immensely tall; in any case, they should be bigger than normal human size. The details of the visualization are left to your individual intuition and imagination. One fellow recently wrote a letter to a well-known magician asking what color eyes and hair the archangels should have. It is possible to work this out logically based on the elemental associations, but the simple answer is, "Whatever color they are when the angels appear to you in your imagination."

When you say "Before me flames the pentagram," extend your legs out to each side so that your body approximates the shape of a pentagram, and visualize a pentagram of white light vibrating within your body.

Some people prefer to say, "Within me flames the pentagram and in the column shines the six-rayed star." This is based on a variation introduced by Aleister Crowley; the other version is that used by the Stella Matutina, an off-shoot of the Golden Dawn.

Finally, repeat the qabalistic cross ("Ateh" through "Amen," as explained previously). You should experience a feeling of peace and wholeness.

Now you are ready to begin your practice. Sit in a comfortable chair in the center of the room and, if necessary, repeat your relaxation routine. Then close your eyes and visualize one of the Tarot cards in front of you. It should be the size of a door and should be placed against the wall of the room. It is better to use one of the trumps to begin with, but later you can experiment with the Minor Arcana.

When you have the card clearly visualized and as vivid and steady as possible, imagine yourself getting up and standing before the card. If you have any experience at astral projection, you may prefer to formulate your body of light and step into it, or simply do so in your imagination. (There is a very fine line here between imagining stepping into your astral body and actually doing so. There *is* a difference, however.)

When you are standing in front of the card and have everything well visualized, simply step into the card as if you were stepping through an open doorway.

What happens next depends upon the nature of your pathworking. If you are actually working a path of the Tree of Life, you may choose to vibrate an appropriate God name and/or angelic name, and to trace the appropriate figures in the air. These are techniques for trained magicians, however; the novice need not trouble himself/herself about such fine points.

You may then venture off into the landscape, begin a conversation with any figures that happen to be present, or wait for a guide to show up. A guide can be very helpful, but I know of no one who has been eternally trapped in a card because they did not wait for a guide.

Once your adventure or learning experience is over with, return to your starting point and step out of the card and back into your body. Allow yourself to return slowly to normal consciousness. Preferably, perform the protection ritual a second time (it only takes about five minutes). Walk around or have a bite to eat

The Hanged Man from The New Golden Dawn Ritual Tarot

to "ground" yourself—that is, to fully return yourself to normal awareness so that you are not walking around "spaced out"—and then record your experience in a journal you have acquired for the purpose.

What deck should you use for pathworking? The answer to that is simple: whichever one you like! Whereas a deck must have certain characteristics that make it suitable for some of the other uses of Tarot, the restrictions for choosing a deck for pathworking are practically nil. The choice is very much an individual matter and depends entirely on your purposes.

Many people may find it difficult to carry out an imaginative journey with a card that is drawn in an artistic style other than realism, such as the art nouveau of the Crowley deck or the cubism of the Cicero deck. Others may have no problem with that, but may feel uncomfortable with a deck that is drawn in a style that is realistic in intent but poorly executed in practice, with crudely drawn, poorly proportioned figures. Still others may prefer one of the more abstract designs to spark the imagination. There are decks that might have a tendency to make you feel as if you were in a comic book or in some adolescent boy's sex fantasy. It is impossible to do useful pathworking with such a deck.

Judgment from the Witches Tarot

If you wish to perform formal pathworkings in the Golden Dawn magical qabalistic tradition, you will need a deck that recognizes the qabalistic associations and Golden Dawn correspondences and that is designed with these in mind. The ideal deck in this case would probably be the New Golden Dawn Ritual Tarot by Sandra Tabatha Cicero (Llewellyn Publications, 1991). The symbolism and coloration of this deck are detailed and correct. Alternately, there is the Golden Dawn Tarot designed by Robert Wang, which, despite the fact that the figures are somewhat crudely drawn, is a very powerful deck.

If you have no particular interest in the Golden Dawn or in qabalah, you may prefer a deck that is designed around whichever tradition you prefer. There is no shortage of Tarot decks, so the difficulty of finding such a deck should be almost nonexistent. Many Wiccans may be comfortable with Ellen Cannon Reed's Witches Tarot Deck drawn by Martin Cannon, or they may prefer the elegantly drawn Robin Wood Tarot. The Robin Wood Tarot is based on the designs of Pamela Colman Smith's Rider-Waite deck, but there are important variations that make it less useful for the Golden Dawn aficionado than some of the other decks. At the

The Six of Swords from the Robin Wood Tarot

same time, it incorporates a great many Pagan elements and will naturally appeal to Pagans much more than any deck that is more tailored to the Rosicrucian or high magic tradition. Thelemites will usually prefer the Thoth deck of Aleister Crowley.

There are also decks designed specifically for the Norse, Greek, Arthurian, Celtic, and Egyptian traditions—and just about any other tradition you can name, including the Candomblé tradition of Africa, exemplified in the Tarot of the Orishas published by Llewellyn. Those with an African heritage might prefer this deck, whereas people with a Celtic background—or just a British heritage in general— might well find the greatest attraction in Legend: The Arthurian Tarot, exquisitely designed and illustrated by Anna Marie Ferguson. These images can evoke ancestral memories and what one might call "genetic nostalgia" even when the dry, antiquated narratives of Geoffrey of Monmouth leave one yawning.

Speaking personally, even though I do not consider myself a Thelemite or agree with Crowley's cosmology or eschatology, I have found the best (most interesting, most informative) pathworking experiences to be associated with the Crowley deck. The symbolism and detail are sufficiently rich to spark my imagination and lead into some very interesting byways.

This preference, however, extends only to the Major Arcana. There are also some fascinating experiences to be had with the Minor Arcana of the Robin Wood deck.

Following are some examples of pathworking using the Tarot. These workings represent the experiences of several different people, although they have all been edited and rewritten in my own words for the sake of clarity and consistency. The first is rather short and consists primarily of a conversation. You may find that this is true of many of your early pathworkings.

Robin Wood Deck—The Emperor

I step across the threshold—taking care not to trip on the banner emblazoned with the name of the card—and find myself facing a kindly, wise, middle-aged man. He nods, encouraging me to speak. I remember that one should not address royalty without being spoken to first, so I respectfully remain silent.

"How may I serve you?" he says, as if sensing the reason for my hesitation.

"Your majesty," I say, "you are an emperor. It is not for you to serve me, surely!"

"Yes," he says. "It is the function of every ruler to serve his subjects. He has no other purpose. It is true that this service demands leadership, courage, and confidence, and even the ability to be stern when it is necessary. Woe unto him who incurs the wrath of an emperor! But even then, that wrath is on behalf of the people he rules; it is not on his own account."

"Where I come from," I tell him, "rulers often lack this wisdom."

"Then," he says, "they are not kings. They are tyrants."

"The law of the jungle," I say. "Survival of the fittest."

"No," he says. "Survival of the strongest. It is not the same thing."

As I reflect on this, my eyes wander over his majestic figure. In spite on his kindness and friendliness, I find him a little intimidating. I wonder about his scepter.

"Tell me, your majesty," I say, "why do you bear the emblem of Venus on your scepter? I have been told that you rule in the sign of the Ram, and, indeed, the designs on your throne would seem to bear that out."

The Emperor, from the Robin Wood Deck

"It is the crux ansata, the Egyptian cross of life," he says, "just as Venus is connected with the giving of life. The life of this world is under my dominion, to give through spiritual fathership or to take away by my command."

"Is that a wreath of holly I see on your brow?" I inquire.

"I know what you are thinking," he says, "but no, I am not that One. The wreath is of laurel, sacred to Apollo, and signifies rulership. You need to study botany."

"There seems little chance for that here," I say. "The landscape seems so barren!"

"Just as reason untempered by love is barren," he says. "But do not be deceived by appearances. Even an apparently desolate landscape can be teeming with life unseen. And in those mountains, by a way that requires both courage and the clarity of logic to assay, is my palace, which you must visit some day."

"May I do so now?" I ask.

"I do not think you are ready for that yet," he says. "In the outward world, this fact is signified by the demands on your time. That casserole has been in the oven long enough!"

He lifts his hand in dismissal. I bow my head and step backwards out of the card.

Thoth Deck—Death

With some trepidation, I pass through the doorway and stand behind the dancing, cavorting, thrashing figure of Death Himself.

I hesitate to accost the gyrating skeleton. Even though I know that Death is nothing but transformation, and indeed I seek a transformative experience, I have no overpowering desire to die.

Without warning, the figure whirls and confronts me, the grinning, blackened skull staring me right in the face, inches away.

"Fear is failure and the forerunner of fifty-five fools!" screams the skull. The voice is harsh, high-pitched, hysterical, like a speed-freak I once encountered on the street in Berkeley in the early '70s.

I summon my courage and give the Thelemic greeting: "Do what thou wilt shall be the whole of the Law."

The Death figure instantly changes into that of an attractive young woman wearing nothing at all. "Love is the law, love under will," she says in a breathy voice. I am inclined to smile at her, but I am afraid. I am all too acutely aware of what she was an instant before.

"My embrace is ... DEATH!" she cries. At the beginning of the sentence, she is still the young woman, but her voice becomes harsher and shriller until, at the final word, she stands with legs apart, arms flung out in the position of Set triumphant, her body that of the rotting corpse of a crone. Then she shrieks and cackles with a seemingly endless insane laughter.

She is now the skeleton again, taking up the scythe once more.

"Fear not the bite of the scorpion," says the skull.

Even though I am still leery of both the scorpion and the serpent that crawls along the ground to my left, I seem to be in no danger from them. They are ignoring me. As I watch, however, the scorpion stings itself. It writhes and dies, then begins immediately to rot and putrefy. The odor is atrocious. But now the "mass of loathsome, of detestable putrescence" sinks into the soil, and the pale green shoots of new plants break through the surface. Time seems speeded up, for the plants rapidly mature into prickly pear cacti with the blooms of blue-green flowers upon them.

Meanwhile, the figure of Death has moved away. I see it still reaping lives with its great scythe, but now it is in the distance.

Although I have been wary of the serpent (which I do not see any longer) and the

Death, from the Crowley-Harris Thoth Tarot

scorpion, I have more or less ignored the large, bloated fish which has been swimming about through the air all this time. Now I see that I have been wrong to do so, for it suddenly swims toward me and—although much too small to do so—opens its huge mouth, engulfs me, and swallows me!

The experience is nothing like what I have imagined of Jonah and the whale, and it certainly does not resemble Pinocchio and Giapetto in the belly of Monstro the Whale in the Disney film. It is pitch dark, and I am held in the hot, slimy belly of the fish, unable to move because of the tight, suffocating restriction. I consider making the necessary effort to break off the pathworking despite the known after-effects that the shock of a sudden return to normal consciousness would involve. After all, how long is it going to be before the fish begins to digest me?

It is difficult to explain what follows because I can see and hear nothing; I am still enveloped in the stomach of the fish. Nevertheless, I can sense things that are happening on the outside. I sense the fish being caught in a net and dragged into a boat. I sense the boat coming to a dock and the net being removed with the fish in it. I sense the fish being dumped on the ground, and then a hole being dug and the fish kicked in the hole. The fish is buried alive. Then all is quiet.

I do not know how long it takes for all this to happen, because I am in a state approaching deep meditation—or possibly sleep—but I begin to become alarmed after the fish has been buried and nothing seems to happen for a long while. But then I am aware that I am standing up, regardless of my own volition, bursting through the fish and the soil and standing naked in the sunlight! I have been reborn.

Not far way, I see the figure of Death, still reaping with its scythe. But now I notice a fish-net hung at its waist.

I find that I am near the point where I began my journey, so I turn and exit the card.

Haindl Deck—The Hermit

The deck painted by Hermann Haindl (U.S. Games, 1990) is very interesting; it features suggestive, impressionistic images that make it an apt candidate for pathworking experiences. The example pathworking follows.

I enter the card in the usual manner. My first intention is to speak to the figure of the

Hermit, who stands some little distance away up a rocky slope. Two large birds are between me and him; they seem to bar the way. Another huge bird is coming down for a landing behind the Hermit. It is as if they are attracted by his lantern. The peering faces of gnomes appear from behind the rocks.

To my surprise, the giant birds merely regard me curiously as I approach the Hermit. The gnomes vanish into hiding. The gray, damp rock of the landscape is hard and cold under my bare feet as I walk. Then I stand before the figure.

But the Hermit pays even less attention to me than the birds do! He is rapt in some sort of ecstatic trance, and I have the feeling that nothing I could do or say would attract his slightest notice.

Such being the case, for lack of anything better to do, I address one of the birds.

"Does he stay this way for very long at a time?" I ask the nearest bird.

The bird looks quizzically at me but says nothing.

Perhaps the bird will now seize me in its talons and carry me off to another adventure. No? Then it appears that I must make my way down the mountain. There is nothing that I can do here except wait—perhaps indefinitely—for

The Hermit

The Hermit from the Haindl Deck

the Hermit to come out of his trance. In fact, I realize, he may never do so.

I begin my descent of the mountain. If there is a trail, it is not very clear, although one way or another seems to make for easier going. It is rather cold, and even though the breeze is very light, it cuts through to the bone. There is moisture in the air, and I become aware of the fact that some of the rock surfaces are coated with a thin sheet of ice. I cannot see more than a few yards in any direction because of the thick fog that envelops everything.

The Hermit—superior and authoritative and aloof—just like my father. I can remember wanting him to play some game with me when I was a small child, but he was watching news of the Viet Nam war on television and kept telling me to be quiet and listen—as if any of it could mean anything to me at my age. I was never able to get through to him, and it seems as if I will never be able to get through to the Hermit, either.

Feeling alone and lost, I continue the descent. When will I come out below the clouds, or does this fog extend all the way to the valley below? Will I meet the Fool coming up?

As I climb down upon a flat, gray rock, I see a small, round gemstone that is deep green in color. I have no pockets in my robe, but I decide to carry the stone for good luck. Already, I feel more optimistic. Can it be the effect of the gemstone?

Rounding a corner of what now appears to be a distinct mountain trail, I am astonished to come face to face with the figure of a young girl in a long white dress. She holds a lily in both hands. She does not seem surprised to see me. Instead, her face breaks into a smile.

"I think you're going the wrong way," she says.

"But there's nothing up there but some giant birds and an old man who won't speak to me," I say.

"Did you speak to him?" she asks.

"Well, no; but it was obvious that he was in a deep trance."

"He beckons to you. Look." She points up the mountainside. Surely we are too far down the mountain to be able to actually see the Hermit.

I glance in the direction she is pointing, and I see, dimly but distinctly, the Hermit's lantern shining through the fog.

"Then I should retrace my steps?" I ask.

"No seeker ever comes down the mountain," she says, "not unless it is darkness and dissolution that is sought."

I see that I really have no choice but to go back up the mountain to the Hermit, even though the prospect seems bleak and hopeless. I sigh, turn, and begin climbing back up the mountain.

As I climb, I am surprised to notice that I recognize individual rocks and features in the barren, gray landscape. Even so, I think I would get lost if the beacon of the Hermit's lantern did not indicate the proper direction.

After what seems to be a long time, I reach the Hermit again. The birds are sitting some distance behind him. They seem to be asleep. The Hermit still appears not to notice me, but I approach him anyway.

"Sir," I say, "is this indeed the end of the path?"

The Hermit, whose arms are outspread as if beholding a vision in the heavens, suddenly looks at me and puts his arm around my shoulders.

"Yes, it is," he says, "but I daresay it looks very different to you than it does to me. To achieve the final vision of reality itself, you must devote long years to spiritual disciplines. You cannot achieve enlightenment through one journey of your imagination, or with many. But seek, and you shall find. Seek. Seek. Seek. And keep ever the light of the lantern before you."

"It is hard," I say.

"It may seem so," he says. "But you must persist."

"Thank you," I say, and turn to go. I know that I will persist on the path.

"One more thing," he says. "None of this has anything to do with your father. That is a different matter entirely, and it begins with love."

The Hermit seems to fade into the fog as I find myself drifting out of the card and back into my chair. The journey is over.

Tarot of Marseilles—The Lover

The Tarot of Marseilles is one of the oldest existing complete decks. It was probably the most readily available Tarot deck before the Rider-Waite deck was published. Some writers recommend it as the preferred deck because its age supposedly makes it closer to some hypothetical original.

Be that as it may, the sixth Trump differs both from most modern versions and from the oldest medieval versions: it shows a young man between an older woman and a younger one, with Cupid hovering overhead about to loose his arrow at the young man. The standard, exoteric interpretation is that the older woman on the young man's right side represents virtue, while the younger woman represents vice. The oldest versions of this card, however, show only one man and one woman, with Cupid uniting them in love. Modern decks are more apt to follow Waite's lead and show one man and one woman with an angel hovering overhead. Golden Dawn versions show the myth of Perseus and Andromeda, which signifies the rescue of the aspirant from the lower passions of the reptilian brain by her/his higher self—a far cry from the homely scene of the Tarot of Marseilles. Following is the narrative of a path-working scenario.

When I step into the card, everyone is talking at once. I cannot make out what anyone is saying with any clarity, but it would seem that both women are trying to convince the young man to marry them while he is hemming and hawing and trying to avoid a decision. Meanwhile, Cupid hovers overhead trying to keep the man in his sights as he turns from side to side or steps back or forward. I have the feeling that the young man will decide in favor of whichever woman he is facing when he is struck by the arrow.

The older woman is telling the youth that she is a good cook and housekeeper—there are

*The Lovers from a nineteenth-century French deck similar to
the Tarot of Marseilles*

no liberated women in this medieval scene—and will be a faithful companion. The younger is trying to convince him that she is the better prospect to bear his children as well as being more attractive to look at. The young man appears to be agreeing with both of them in turn, but he really can't make up his mind.

I expect Cupid to fire his arrow and decide the issue, but he keeps wavering as if he can't decide who to aim at. Meanwhile, the discussion among the three figures continues without making any progress. Bored, I decide to walk around and see what else I can find.

The landscape is rural. Farmland stretches away on all sides with small copses of trees here and there. No buildings are in sight, although the countryside is fairly flat. I am following a narrow but distinct path. It is warm, but not hot, and the time seems to be early afternoon.

Right away, I find myself at a fork in the path. There does not appear to be any reason why I should go one way rather than the other, so I just stand there pondering.

Then, quite suddenly, I find an older and somewhat ugly woman on my right hand and a younger and quite attractive woman on my left. Now I am the young man, and I know that an

The Lovers from Legend: The Arthurian Tarot

invisible Cupid hovers overhead. Now I no longer get to stand aside and be a disinterested witness. Now the decision is mine.

It's any easy one for me. The young woman is a fox. The older lady is no doubt a very wise crone, but she is still a crone as far as I am concerned. These are modern times, after all, and I feel that I do not need to be concerned about antique notions of virtue versus vice. I will take the dare.

I take the hand of the younger woman, and she leads me down the left-hand path.

We haven't gone ten paces before a really disgusting demon rises up through the ground directly in our path. He is a repulsive shade of greenish orange and looks fat and slimy. I do not like the way he is smiling at us with those huge fangs.

I grasp the hand of the young woman harder than before and prepare to turn and run, but she says, "Ah, there you are. Here's another one for you."

She breaks free of my grip and runs to the demon. She fawns upon him, and he puts a slimy arm around her.

"Soon you will be the one with the horns!" says the demon, and breaks into a horrible cackle.

Filled with anger and disappointment that I cannot control even the events happening, after all, in my own imagination, but unwilling to break off the working abruptly as if awakening from a nightmare, I turn to run. I find myself facing the older woman whom I'd left standing at the crossroads.

"If you judge by superficialities and make such a choice in your worldly life," she says, "the demons you meet will have a different aspect, but they will still be there. You find me unattractive, but I suggest you remember some of the crone figures in folklore and the changes they underwent after they had been accepted for their inner worth. Meanwhile, be glad you have used this pathworking rather than your life to discover your folly."

Of course, no figure in a pathworking can tell you something you don't already know, I think, but we don't always keep all the world's wise advice in consciousness. Chastened, I thank the lady and silently and slowly walk out of the card and go back to sitting in my room. I will have something to think about.

New Golden Dawn Ritual Tarot— The Star

After robing and performing the Lessor Banishing Ritual of the Pentagram, I sit facing the actual constellation of Aquarius in the sky and go though my relaxation ritual once again. When I feel ready, I begin to visualize the card. After a few minutes, it is perfectly clear in all its detail—staring at it ahead of time helps a great deal. I formulate my Body of Light and transfer into it. Then I concentrate on the image of the card again to fix its details and bring it out vividly. When everything is in order, I step through the portal into the card.

Unfortunately, the card seems to be constructed in such a way that I immediately step up to my knees in the pool of water! I suppose I could have foreseen this and made arrangements to walk on the water to dry land. Nevertheless, I trace the invoking pentagram of Air and vibrate ORO IBAH AOZPI, then trace the sign of Aquarius in its center and vibrate YOD-HEH-VAV-HEH. The image of the central figure, the Goddess, becomes more vivid, less stylized, and more human.

I hear water gurgling. The Goddess does not acknowledge my presence. I see an armored figure approaching. When he comes closer, I see that he is riding a black horse, has a visored helm that hides his face, and wears a dark red-orange surcoat emblazoned with a red cross. He dismounts and doffs his helm. He is a blond man in his 30s.

"Good day to you, sir," he says, and then kneels to speak with the Goddess.

I look around. I stand under a night sky with a single seven-pointed star blazing away in the west.

Towards the north are mountains as before [refers to a previous pathworking with this card], but now I perceive a town of nondescript color perched on a hillside. There is a road or path leading to it. To the east of that is the river, beyond which is a dark plain with isolated trees silhouetted against the night sky. To the east, I see a goddess standing on the plain across the river, perhaps a hundred feet away. She wears a feathered headdress and has a gown made of white feathers. The plain extends around to the west, where I see the river run into a bay with a distant town on it. So we are upstream (I think) from my previous visions.

I now see, standing under a tree, the knight's page, a young blond woman holding his horse and lance.

The Star from the New Golden Dawn Ritual Tarot

"Hello," she says (unprompted). "My name is Silaina."

I don't get the name at first. "Sally?" I say.

"No, Silaina," says the Goddess [the central figure of the card], who has left the pool and approached. "Have a look around again."

To the west, between and beyond the trees of a forest that grows in that direction, is an amber castle with red-orange roofs, atop a hill.

"What is the meaning of the amber castle?" I ask.

"It is thine." says the Goddess. "Thou hast spent the last thirty years building it."

I look to the north and see the purple mountains and the sea toward the east, and there is a ship with a sail of red and white vertical stripes emblazoned with a black double eagle.

"And the ship?" I say.

"It is thine to use when thou travelest in our realms."

I look to the southwest and see the city on the bay.

"What is that city?"

"It is the city of heavenly peace," says Silaina, the page.

"The city of heavenly peace and celestial joy," says the Goddess. "It is called Geronzin."

I feel that the time I have allotted for this exercise is growing short, and I am beginning to suspect that, despite all my precautions, astral shells are making sport with me, flattering my ego for their own purposes. I thank the Goddess and the page and excuse myself. I leave the card and gradually come out of my dream-like state.

I decide to investigate the word "Geronzin" by gematria. The first number I come up with is 326, which is the same as the name of Yehoshuah, the savior.

Legend: The Arthurian Tarot— Strength

Following my usual method, I shuffle the cards and choose this one at random. This deck is new, and I have not used it before. I am curious as to the results I will get. After studying the card for about five minutes, I shut my eyes, relax, and attempt to visualize it. I have to open my eyes to check details two or three times, but finally I have a clear image of the card before me, projected to the size of a door on the east wall of my bedroom.

I imagine myself getting up and going to the doorway in the wall. I take the time to visualize myself in medieval armor, with my magical sword at my side, in order to fit in with the milieu. I feel a fresh breeze on my skin, and I smell the odor of vegetation—mingled, I suddenly realize, with the smell of a large animal and, less pleasantly, with the odor of a huge reptile. I gingerly step out onto the dry leaves of the forest.

The two women in the card let go of each other's hand and the lion comes to rest on all fours. I am a little intimidated by the fact that both women, the lion, and the giant snake are all looking at me expectantly, just as executives

Strength from Legend: The Arthurian Tarot

at a meeting might stop talking and look at the mail boy when he comes in to deliver a message.

I don't really know what to say, and so silence reigns for a few seconds. Then the lion yawns, licks its chops, and looks away. That seems to be the signal for everyone to go about her business.

The lion wanders off toward the left, still bearing the young woman. The serpent sinks to the ground, and the crone dismounts. Although she is an older woman, she is not in any way repulsive or hideous.

"You must marry me," she says.

I know the legend behind the design of this particular card, and I know that the crone represents the Old Religion. After Percivale slew her serpent (which now, however, appears to be resurrected, or replaced), she demanded that he become her man in recompense. He refused, which was a symbol of his adherence to the Christian faith (symbolized by the lion). Agreeing to becoming involved with the crone would have been the same as renouncing his baptism.

I, however, am under no such restriction. Still, why would I want to marry the crone?

"Why?" I say. "I did not kill your snake."

"I need a champion," she says, "and what better man to be so than my husband?"

"I serve the Goddess already," I reply. "I do not need to marry you or anyone else in order to do so."

"So be it, sir knight," she says.

The crone sighs and gets back on the serpent. As the serpent glides away, the crone waves to me and says, "My blessing on those who serve the Lady."

At this point, the younger woman comes out of the trees and approaches me. The lion is not with her.

"It is I whom you must marry," she says. "Do you not fear the serpent?"

"I fear lions much more," I say.

"The lion will be thy companion, as he was Percivale's," she says.

"I have met those who have lions for companions," I say. (I am taking "those who have lions" to be an allegory for "Christians," particularly the proselytizing variety.) "They are unpleasant and often dangerous."

"Dangerous only to those who serve the Evil One!" cries the young woman. "And so, if you will be the devil's knight, I'll have none of you!"

She flounces off into the forest again.

"There is no devil!" I call after her, but she is gone.

Now I am alone in the forest—no women, no snakes, no lions. There is no sign of any other living creature except for the song of a bird. Is there some lesson of this card that I have failed to learn by not taking the right action? But I am not prepared to marry anyone in a Tarot card—or in "real life," for that matter.

"They are both part of you," says a man's voice close behind me.

I whirl, hand to the hilt of my sword, and see an old man in a wizard's robes standing a few feet away leaning on a staff.

"You cannot refuse to marry either one of those woman," says the wizard. "They are both already part of you—the best part of Paganism and the best part of Christianity—aye, and the worst parts, too, but deeper hidden. It is well enough that you serve the Goddess, 'sir knight,' but do not be intolerant of those who do not share your wisdom."

"If they are part of me already," I reply, "then I am already married to them. Why, then, do they each claim that I must marry them afresh?"

"What they aim for is not so much marriage in itself," replies the sage, "as recognition of the tie that already exists. You must not disdain either one, as if you were better than they. How can you be better than yourself?"

"How shall I call them back, then?" I say.

"By self-examination," says the wizard. "Your time here is now at an end, and you must leave. When you next adventure in these parts, you may perhaps then have the opportunity to change things. Farewell."

Without even voluntarily leaving the card, I suddenly find myself sitting back in my room. I feel as if I am just waking up after a long nap. It is a long time before I feel normal again.

Enochian Tarot—LEA

It has been noted elsewhere that the Enochian Tarot—designed by Gerald and Betty Schueler and painted by Sallie Ann Glassman—does not coincide with usual Tarot concepts; i.e., it is not a deck of 78 cards including 22 Trumps, 16 face cards, and 40 numbered cards, and the Trumps are not those of, for example, the Rider-Waite deck. Nevertheless, the dreamy, evocative images of these cards make them an excellent choice for pathworking, particularly if you are interested in the Enochian system of magic.

You may choose to use the Enochian variation of the Lesser Banishing Ritual of the Pentagram when you use the Enochian Tarot for pathworking, although this is not strictly necessary. Aleister Crowley most likely used the

16. LEA

THE HIGHER SELF

LEA from the Enochian Tarot

traditional form of the ritual when he did his famous series of astral pathworkings with the Enochian Aires in Africa in 1909. Nevertheless, Gerald and Betty Schueler have described an Enochian version of the ritual that may be preferred by some. (There is no record of what protection rituals, if any, were used by John Dee and Edward Kelly in their sixteenthth-century discovery of the Enochian system.) The Enochian pentagram ritual is described in several books by the Schuelers, but it may be briefly described by saying that the words for the Qabalistic cross are ZAH ONDOH MIH BUZD PAID rather than *Ateh malkuth ve-geburah ve-gedullah le-olahm; amen.* The God names in the quarters are EXARP, HCOMA, NANTA, and BITOM rather than Yod-Heh-Vav-Heh, Adonai, Eheieh, and Agla. The archangels, rather than being Raphael, Gabriel, Michael, and Uriel, are IKZHIKAL, EDLPRNAA, BATAIVAH, and RAAGIOSL.

There are as many versions of the correct pronunciation of Enochian as there are people who have written on the subject, so I will not go into that here. It is easy to consult any of the many excellent books that discuss the subject, such as *The Golden Dawn* by Israel Regardie and any of the Enochian books written by Gerald and Betty Schueler, such as *Enochian Magic* or *The Enochian Workbook*.

Depending upon the card used, you should also recite the appropriate Enochian call. The choice of a call is described in detail on page 72 of *Enochian Magic* by the Schuelers.

In this particular case, we are investigating a card of the Major Arcana, which in this deck represents one of the 30 Aethyrs. LEA (pronounced "leh-ah") is the 16th Aethyr. This pathworking—or Aethyr-working, properly speaking—is given as an example only. Those inexperienced with the Enochian system should always begin with the lowest Aethyr, TEX. It has been my experience that warnings about magical effects or the dangers of certain magical systems are usually grossly exaggerated and that even a rank amateur can proceed with impunity (and probably with no effect at all). This is not true of the Enochian system. These spirits are for real, and they can and will kick butt.

After performing the protection ritual and reciting the call of the Aethyr in Enochian, I stare at the card for awhile and then relax and close my eyes.

The figure of a king approaches.

"Hey, buddy," he says, "just a little friendly warning, here." He puts one arm around me. He needs a bath. He is drunk; his breath reeks.

"That bitch coming yonder," he says, "now that's what they mean when they say 'Feminazi.' Don't mess with her unless you want your face eaten off."

I look down the narrow mountain path and see an extremely beautiful and erotic woman riding naked upon a bull and approaching our position.

"Make way!" she cries. "Ring in the new and ring out the old!"

"Oh, shoot! She's here!" says the king. He tosses his scepter over the precipice and throws his cup and crown into the dirt. He slides out of his ermine robe and stands there in soiled white long johns. Without further word, he dives over the cliff and disappears into the swirling mist.

"Thus passes the Age of Iron," says the woman, now sitting on the bull next to where I stand. She dismounts and picks up the cup dropped by the king. The bull snorts.

"What do you most desire?" she says.

"You," I say. Under the circumstances, and considering the allure of this lady, I believe I would speak similarly even if I were not conscious that this is a working and not a situation in the so-called real world. And, after all, she is the figure of Lust personified.

She laughs. "You would be utterly consumed by my glory!" she says. "Think of the consequences before you speak, or be heedless and be dead. In your present blind condition, what do you most desire?"

"Uh—knowledge," I say.

"Then know this!" she says. "There is nothing that you can know. To know anything at all is to know something wrong. There is no such thing as absolute truth and therefore no such thing as true knowledge. Authorial intent is irrelevant to the meaning of a text! All is chaos! Entropy is Lord! Matter is exalted above Spirit, and existence precedes essence! Chaos, chaos, saith the Lordy!"

She begins to laugh hysterically as the bull plunges over the cliff, a bolt of lightning strikes the mountainside above our heads, rocks fly everywhere, an unseen horse whinnies in panic, and a man wearing a Shriner fez hurtles down the path doing cartwheels and goes on over the cliff after the bull, snickering like a fool and all the while shouting "Iä! Iä! Shub Niggurath! The goat with a thousand young!"

"You see?" she cries. "When the monarch plunged into the abyss, he went to his death. When the bull leaped over, he leapt into manifestation and glory! When the clown fell, he fell into oblivion! Will you leap? Which will it be for you? Go ahead! Jump! Find out!"

Before I can speak or make a move of any kind, I find myself instantly in an eighteenth-century drawing room watching a string quartet play something by Mozart. I believe it is the "Dissonance Quartet." The walls themselves are sky blue, but the woodwork and trim is all white. The musicians all have wigs and period costumes.

Then I suddenly notice that the cello player is the naked woman, who is Babalon. She winks at me, and I find myself sitting in my own chair in my own room. I hear crickets chirping outside. The working has ended without my volition.

It ought to go without saying that many pathworkings, perhaps even most of them, are much more elaborate than the little scenarios presented here. Most of them involve extensive traveling from the spot where the card is entered, particularly if they are formal pathworkings in connection with the qabalistic Tree of Life. Donald Michael Kraig provides a more detailed example in his book, *Modern Magick* (Llewellyn, 1988). Dolores Ashcroft-Nowicki has written at least two books on the subject (Aquarian Press), but they are not specifically related to using the Tarot as a starting point. The best thing for you to do is to sit down with your chosen deck and try it yourself.

Good traveling!

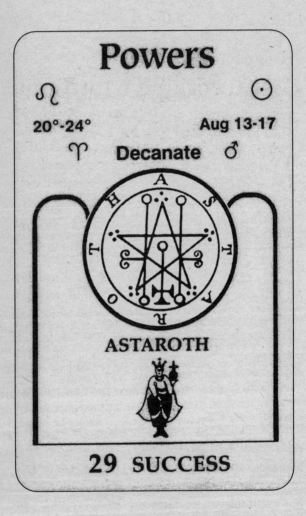

Powers

♌   ☉

20°-24°   Aug 13-17

♈   **Decanate**   ♂

ASTAROTH

29 SUCCESS

Astaroth, from the Solomon Deck

❧ 6 ❧

Dreamworking with Tarot

Dreamworking is very similar to pathworking, but the procedure is somewhat more involved. As many dabblers have discovered to their dismay, dreamwork is not quite as simple and easy as some magazine articles might lead you to believe. It is not really difficult, but it does require determination and persistence.

The foundation for the practice of dreamworking is to be found among cultures that retain something of their primordial tradition. Thanks to Frank G. Speck, whose work was popularized by Marie-Louise von Franz, it is well known that the Naskapi tribe of Labrador ordinarily pays great attention to their dreams and consciously uses them to solve daily problems. Usually these are not the sorts of problems that we might think of in this connection. The Naskapi do not ask "How can I succeed in my business?" or even "How can I advance upon my spiritual path?" They are far more likely to ask questions such as, "Where is the most plentiful game?" or "Where is the best place to fish tomorrow?" or "Will it snow this week?"

The original inhabitants of Australia also place much faith in dreams. They recognize the fact, seemingly rediscovered by modern psychologists, that there is no time in dreams— they take place in eternity. The unconscious mind does not recognize the passage of time. To this part of your mind, whatever happened yesterday is just the same as what you did on your fourth birthday. It is all coexistent in the eternal Now.

Consequently, the Australian myths of the origins of all things take place, not at the creation of the world, but in the "dreamtime." What we call "the beginning" takes place in the eternal Now as God or the gods continually re-create the Universe every picosecond or so. It is important in the tradition of these people, and many others like them, to do things as they were done "in the beginning," in the dreamtime. A myth may describe how a god first planted yams; based on this primordial pattern, everyone knows how to plant yams now. If they deviate from the procedure set down by the god in the eternal dreamtime, the crop will fail.

Reliance on dreams is not confined to "uncivilized" peoples. In classical Greece, a common dream in all strata of society was for a deity to come to the head of your bed and give you advice about important problems. Even without conscious reliance, dreams have proved to be a fertile field of inspiration in science and in all the arts. Both Robert Louis Stevenson and H. P. Lovecraft derived many of their story plots from dreams, and the structures of both the benzene ring and DNA molecules were revealed in dreams to their "discoverers."

An individual living in our contemporary world in a nontraditional society such as that in the United States can approach dreams in a variety of ways and at many different levels of involvement. The first step on any of these paths, however, is to begin remembering and recording your dreams. If you do not habitually remember your dreams, then all the other procedures and exercises and rituals given in books will be useless.

If you plan to use dreamworking for problem solving or personal growth, then the first thing you must do is begin a dream diary. Keep a writing instrument and notepad by your bedside so that you may write down things immediately when you awaken. The memory of dreams normally fades very quickly, and you will forget them if you do not write them down at once. Of course, this may lead to your scratching your head in the morning as you try to decipher your own illegible scrawl made at 3 A.M. in the dark! Still, it is a worthwhile procedure. Just the task of writing them down—legibly or not—will help you to remember your dreams later, and not everything you write will be indecipherable.

If you have written nothing in the night and cannot remember any dreams when you wake up in the morning, enter a notation in your dream diary anyway—"I did not remember any dreams this morning," or words to that effect. Just the act of writing something in your dream diary will stimulate your dream memory.

Once you have begun to remember a fair number of your dreams in reasonable detail, you will be ready to attempt the use of the Tarot for dreamwork.

For this purpose, it is not necessary to become involved in such techniques as "lucid dreaming," though you may do so if you wish. What you will be trying to do with the Tarot is to use it as a problem-solving tool, or an instrument of personal growth, by dreaming about specific cards. In a more general sense, you

"Dancers" from the Buckland
Gypsy Fortunetelling Deck

want to know what a card has to teach you, what lesson it embodies that you need to learn.

You may find that such devices as crystals and dream-catchers will help you to program and remember dreams, but you may also find that you can do without them just as well. Such details are up to you, but you should make your choices based upon experimentation, not whim.

If you are heavily involved with the Tarot during your waking hours for some extended period of time, you may find that you will dream about a Tarot card spontaneously. That seldom happens, however. There are a million and one things that seem more important to the conscious mind than "mere" cards, and these concerns are reflected in the subconscious imagery of dreams. Only if a card symbolizes some important psychic event in a striking, dramatic, and unmistakable fashion is it likely to appear spontaneously.

Accordingly, you will have to "program" yourself to dream about a selected card. The card you choose may simply be one that piques your interest or that seems to hold a hidden message for you. On the other hand, it may be chosen on the basis of its divinatory meaning, or for some other reason, because it is applica-

The Hierophant from Legend: The Arthurian Tarot.

ble to some particular problem for which you wish to seek a solution in dreams.

It may be enough simply to look at the card and tell yourself, "I will dream about this card tonight." In most cases, you will have to do more than that. I would suggest that you relax as much as possible and perhaps meditate a few minutes to establish the suitable conditions, and then stare at the chosen card for about five minutes. Periodically, every ten or twenty seconds or so, you can affirm to yourself that "I will dream about this card tonight." Then close your eyes and try to visualize the card. Do not at this time experiment with daydreaming about the image on the card, and certainly do not attempt any pathworking. Such endeavors will automatically take the place of the dream. Then go immediately to bed and sleep with the card under your pillow, perhaps accompanied by a dream crystal.

Do not be disappointed if you do not dream about the card after all your preparations and good intentions. In fact, it is a bit unlikely that you will actually dream about the card, or the images in the card, on your first attempt. The secret to success in this technique is persistence. If it just does not work even after you have tried it on a dozen consecutive nights, try

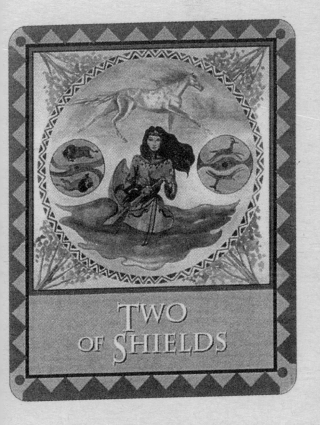

Two of Shields from the Healing Earth Tarot

it on the thirteenth night. Eventually, you will get results.

The results may surprise you. You may not realize right away that a particular dream had anything to do with the card in question. Only when you read over your dreams later and reflect upon them will it become obvious to you. In that case, you have received your answer.

The deck you should use for dreamworking is again a matter of personal choice. You may go strictly by feeling, by "vibes," or you may choose a deck that resonates with your ancestral heritage such as the Tarot of the Orishas, Legend: The Arthurian Tarot, Buckland's Gypsy Fortunetelling Deck, or the Norse Tarot. My own choice for dreamworking is the Healing Earth Tarot of Jyoti and David McKie. I will admit that I am prejudiced in this direction, because the image of the Fool as depicted in this deck appeared to me in a dream four years before I ever saw the deck and long before I ever had any contact with the creators. The only difference is that, in my dream, the Fool appeared on a surfboard, flying above the earth like the Silver Surfer of the comic books. In the actual card, the dog is in the same position as the front half of the surfboard in my dream.

The Fool from the Healing Earth Tarot

The Healing Earth Tarot offers a rich source of material for dreamwork because of its eclectic design. It is both contemporary and traditional at the same time. The cards correspond to a variety of cultures: Native American, Australian, African, Chinese, South American, ancient European, and so on. There are the usual 22 Trumps, but the face cards are uniquely called Grandmother, Grandfather, Woman, and Man. There are six suits: Shields (Earth), Rainbows (Water), Wands (Fire), Crystals (Air), Pipes (Wood), and Feathers (Ether). Whereas a deck that is restricted to one culture, one mythology, or one world view might place unnecessary limits on your subconscious mind, the Healing Earth Tarot does not. I certainly cannot dictate to you what your choice should be, but I think you should consider my reasons for making this choice before you make your own.

Sweet dreams.

❧ 7 ❧

Magic with Tarot

Somewhat akin to the use of the cards in meditation in order to achieve a result is their use in ceremonial magic. The use of the Tarot in magic may not be immediately obvious. True, individual cards were used for instruction in some of the grade rituals of the Hermetic Order of the Golden Dawn, but how can a card be part of an actual magical ritual? In fact, the cards can be used as anything from a simple mnemonic device on the order of incense or color to actual talismans.

Not too many years ago (1988, to be exact), Priscilla Schwei developed a kit called The Wisdom of Solomon the King. This kit included a deck of 72 cards bearing the sigils of the spirits of the Goetia of the Lesser Key of Solomon. Accompanying the deck was a small book (*The Solomon Manual of Divination and Ritual Spells*) telling how to use the cards in simple rituals. The only paraphernalia used besides the cards themselves were a few candles. The card served as a seal and a focus for concentration. The spirits were not actually evoked, but were solicited with various requests. Surprisingly, in view of the simplicity of the rituals, the cards work very well for this purpose.

The Enochian Tarot by Gerald and Betty Schueler, with Sallie Ann Glassman as artist, includes cards for many Enochian angels. There are 30 cards for the Aires or Aethyrs, which constitute the Major Arcana of the deck, and four suits, one for each element (Fire, Water, Air, and Earth). Each suit contains a card for the elemental king, six cards for the seniors, and one card each for the higher sephirothic cross angels, lower sephirothic cross angels, kerubic angels, archangels, ruling angels, lesser angels, and demons. The cards should prove very useful indeed in any attempt to evoke these angels. The procedure could be similar to that used with the Solomon deck, or the cards could be used as aids to visualization and concentration, and as talismans, in a full-blown ceremony of evocation to visible appearance.

Also in 1988, Aquarian Press in England produced *Magick and the Tarot* by Tony Willis along with a deck called the Magickal Tarot, by

45. BATAIVAH

THE KING OF AIR

BATAIVAH from the Enochian Tarot

Anthony Clark. In a sense, this book broke new ground because it was the first publication that told specifically how to use Tarot cards for magical purposes.

In 1991, *Tarot Spells* by Janina Renee was published by Llewellyn. Using the Robin Wood deck as an example in all the rituals, Renee described in detail how to use the cards of the Tarot to achieve virtually any magical purpose. Chic Cicero and Sandra Tabatha Cicero included material on the use of Tarot cards in magic, particularly as talismans, in *The New Golden Dawn Ritual Tarot* (Llewellyn, 1991). "The Tarot's greatest use," they say, "is as a magickal implement which can bring spiritual attainment to one who studies it."

Spiritual attainment is the true aim of magic. Spells performed for mundane purposes such as love or money may be all right in their place, but you will usually find that things of the material sphere can be acquired more easily by mundane methods. I suppose it is "neat" to be able to spend an hour performing a ceremony that results in your getting $50 in the mail unexpectedly, but the chances are you could have come by it with much less difficulty and without the expense of $100 worth of magical implements and accessories.

The Magus from the Magickal Tarot

The Two of Cups, representing a union or marriage,
from the New Golden Dawn Ritual Tarot

As for "love," the other most frequent aim of magical spells, every intelligent person is well aware of the bad karma attached to using magical means to influence the will of another. (Apparently it is all right to do so by nonmagical means. We all do that all the time, every time we try to convince anyone of anything.) Besides, a love that is magically acquired is plastic; it is not natural and wholesome. However, knowledge of all these plain facts does not stop people from trying to hedge the issue by casting spells "to meet the ideal companion" or something of the sort. Again, your time (and money) would be better spent meeting people under normal circumstances. If you are after sex without involvement, try a singles bar. That way you won't have the neighbors complaining about your bellowing the barbarous names of evocation in your thin-walled apartment.

The point of all this pontification is simply to say that magic was originally an integral part of religion, and that it was designed for the purpose of reuniting the microcosm (yourself) with the macrocosm (ultimate reality). The whole law of correspondences in magic has been worked out so that things in the material world can be seen as the analogs of things in the celestial realm, and beyond that on the purely spiritual plane. Since these things are also part of you, the microcosm, then you yourself are the material expression of something higher—something with which you are trying to unite or at least realize by means by magic. It is true that you can use the celestial counterparts of material objects to manipulate those objects in some way beneficial to yourself, but that is a side issue.

But whether you want to cast a spell to get rid of warts or whether you wish to work ceremonial magic for the purpose of self-realization and uniting yourself with your Higher Self and finally with God, the cards of the Tarot can be an invaluable aid.

Which deck to use? Obviously, it has to be one that fits in with your particular style of magic. Since magic is based on correspondences and mnemonic devices, the cards have to contain symbolism with which you are familiar, or with which you are at least comfortable. In that connection, I personally prefer the Robin Wood Tarot. I also tend to like the New Golden Dawn Ritual Tarot for magic, because, although I do not adhere by any means to the Golden Dawn system of magic in its entirety, I am at least somewhat familiar with it and find it consistent with the traditional ceremonial magic of people such as Marsilio Ficino and Cornelius Agrippa. Decks that aim for a medieval appearance, which might be thought of as being more consistent with Renaissance magic, usually end up being too vague and nonspecific in their imagery to be of much help in magic.

Why not the Crowley deck, which was my preference for pathworking? When it comes to the actual practice of magic, the Thoth deck of Aleister Crowley is admirably suited for Thelemic magick, but it is slightly dissonant with any other kind.

The fact is, however, that most Tarot magic ends up being worked with the cards of the Minor Arcana. According to Willis, the Major Arcana is suitable for training in the magical philosophy, whereas the Minor Arcana should be used for practical results (including spiritual endeavors). Such being the case, you may need a deck with pictorial images on the numbered cards rather than just a given number of Wands, Cups, Swords, or Pentacles, which is the case with the Golden Dawn deck(s)—hence my first preference for the Robin Wood deck, the Minor Arcana cards of which are unsurpassed.

To illustrate, a magical spell using Tarot is provided here. However, if this particular endeavor is of interest to you, you should consult some of the books that have been mentioned in this chapter for more detailed information.

Many magical effects can be achieved by simply staring at a card, or by meditating upon it (see the chapter on meditation). Schwei, Willis, and Renee all recommend the use of candles with the cards, along with meditation and in some cases a spoken affirmation or "spell," and that is a good approach. Schwei and Willis seem to concentrate on one card for one purpose at a time, but Renee apparently feels that specific results are better obtained with combinations of cards that make everything more explicit. However, you may wish to do something even more elaborate. It would be difficult to achieve more in this direction than the "Tarot Talisman Ritual" given on pages 199–202 of *The New Golden Dawn Ritual Tarot* book. However, that ritual is designed specifically for Golden Dawn magicians with Golden Dawn equipment (Fire Wand, Earth Pentacle, and so on). What I have in mind here is something between the two extremes of just looking at a card by candlelight on the one hand and an

The Four of Swords (The Lord of Rest from Strife), from the
Rider/Waite Tarot

Four of Swords from Legend: The Arthurian Tarot

elaborate Golden Dawn ceremony with full regalia on the other—also something that might have a more universal application.

Suppose you have been involved for some months in some sort of conflict that you have found very stressful. It does not matter what the conflict is; it might have to do with family, friends, business, marriage, social life, or anything else. Suppose you wish to work a spell, not necessarily to end the conflict, but so that you can at least forget about it for a while, so you can retreat and recover without things getting out of hand. In this situation, the ideal card would be the Four of Swords, called by the Golden Dawn the "Lord of Rest from Strife." The Rider/Waite deck and decks based on it show a knight lying on a slab; the first impression is that he is dead. This impression is even greater with the Robin Wood card, where the image looks carved from white stone. In any case, we are assured that the figure is not dead, but only resting deeply.

If you are not already a practicing magician, you will not be equipped with magical tools. However, their use is not really necessary with this ritual. You may use any clean and convenient table for an altar.

Place the card face up on the table. You may light two white candles if you choose; they will help create the proper atmosphere. Place the candles on the table, one to each side.

Take a ritual bath of cleansing, carry out some sort of relaxation routine, and then perform the Lesser Banishing Ritual of the Pentagram (see page 89).

At the conclusion of the pentagram ritual, sit down in a comfortable chair you have placed near the altar. The object of this particular ritual is, after all, "rest." In rituals with other purposes, it might be more appropriate to remain standing.

Stare at the card. It is all right to pick it up and hold it in one hand in order to do this, although it might be easier to prop it up against something so that you don't have to extend the effort of holding your arm up.

You will have to be original in making up some sort of affirmation or "invocation" at this point. The spell will be much more effective if you do. However, it will not be useless even if you omit any spoken words and merely concentrate on the card for a few minutes.

In this particular case, you might say something like this:

O Lord of Rest from Strife, my life has been beset with worries and troubles so that I rest not, I sleep not well, my stomach rumbles under the mildest of food when I can eat at all, and I am sorely distressed. By thy power and thy magic, give me rest and respite from the conflict which has so disturbed my equilibrium, cause the parties involved to speak not to me of the issue, give me surcease and rest, let me sleep like the dead and wake like the resurrected, settle my appetite and my digestion, take away my distress. By Jupiter in Libra, which thou dost in part signify, resolve the contest and stop the whirl of my brain by thy divine authority and balance. In the name of ———— [name of your favored deity, or one chosen as being appropriate], let there be rest from strife. So mote it be.

Continue to look at the card for a few minutes. Then stand up and perform the pentagram ritual once more. Put the card away and return the room to its normal appearance. Then try to forget all about it. Obsessing about the spell will tend to prevent it from working.

Aside from using Tarot cards in such a direct manner to achieve certain results, they can be used in a more incidental manner in other spells simply as one of several mnemonic,

The Tower from Legend: The Arthurian Tarot

associative devices. For example, a spell for spiritual enlightenment might involve a great deal of sun imagery—yellow furnishings, yellow or orange candles, a bit of topaz or olivine and a sunflower on the altar, a drawing or statuette of a lion, another of the Greek god Apollo, frankincense burning on the censer (or a burning stick of incense)—and Tarot trump XIX—The Sun.

Like anything else in magic, the use of Tarot cards in your workings is limited only by your imagination.

Two of Spears from Legend: The Arthurian Tarot

❧ 8 ❧

Collecting Tarot

There are so many attractive decks nowadays, catering to so many different tastes and containing such a tremendous variety of artwork, that you may wish to collect Tarot decks, irrespective of what other uses you may put them to.

Although many Tarot readers and experts frown upon what appears to them to be the mindless accumulation of Tarot decks, as if the purchaser never could decide upon one or two ideal decks, the fact is that selectively collecting Tarot decks can be a rewarding hobby. It may seem expensive at first, since the average deck costs between $20 and $40, but that sum is less than you might spend on many other hobbies such as golf or stamp collecting. And the object you acquire—a deck of cards—is much more interesting and useful than a stamp, a plate, or a pewter figure.

You might choose to specialize in your collection, so that you collect only decks of historical or esoteric importance such as the Tarot of

Marseilles and the Rider-Waite deck. Or you might choose to collect decks that are visually and aesthetically attractive to you. It would be possible to specialize in decks designed around particular traditions, such as those dealing with Norse mythology and the runes. You might confine yourself to decks that adhere to the pattern of the "real" Tarot: 78 cards consisting of 22 trumps, 16 court cards, and 40 numbered cards, with the trumps approximating those in traditional decks. Or, you might decide to specialize in decks that do not adhere to this pattern. Another possibility, and the one that is taken up by most collectors of Tarot, is to grab every one that catches your eye because of esthetic value or esoteric interest. Tarot decks, for the most part, are collections of interesting and attractive pictures. There is no reason, beyond financial limitations, why you should not acquire any of them that appeal to you in any way.

If you want to gloat over your collection, or arrange a temporary display for visual interest in a room, you can pick out various representations of the same card in a variety of different decks and place them under glass on a table, or frame them in groups. The uses you might make of a Tarot collection are limited only by your imagination.

Eventually, you may want to design your own Tarot deck. If you do, blank cards are available for the purpose.

It is possible, of course, to limit your Tarot involvement to collecting decks. However, you will undoubtedly find that the rewards are much greater if you use them for one or more of the other purposes described in this book.

Now we come to confession time: over the years, I have collected nearly 50 decks for various reasons. If I had it to do over again, there are probably as many as five or six that I would not bother to collect—not a bad average. In no particular order, this little collection includes

Robin Wood deck

Cicero Golden Dawn deck

Hermetic Tarot

Magickal Tarot of Anthony Clark

Salvador Dali deck (unfortunately Dali seems to have been entirely ignorant of the esoteric significance of Tarot)

Wang Golden Dawn deck

Aquarian Tarot

Crowley/Harris Thoth deck (in two sizes)

Voyager Tarot

Rider/Waite deck (by two publishers)

Morgan-Greer deck

Medieval Scapini Tarot

Stairs of Gold Tarot by Tavaglione

Tarot of Marseilles

Brotherhood of Light Egyptian Tarot

Merlin Tarot

Prediction Tarot

Cosmic Tarot by Lösche

Witches Tarot by Ellen Cannon Reed and Martin Cannon

A.G. Müller 1JJ deck

Motherpeace Tarot

Hanson-Roberts deck

Tarot of the Ages

Barbara Walker Tarot

Knapp-Hall deck

BOTA deck (including the Lesser Arcana)

Egipcios Kier deck

Dark Horse Tarot

Enchanted Tarot

Norse Tarot

Mythic Tarot

Sacred Rose Tarot

Royal Fez Moroccan Tarot

Gareth Knight deck

Papus deck

Cagliostro deck

Cary-Yale Visconti Tarocchi deck

Minotarot

"Parlour Sybil"

Karma Cards

Rune Magic Cards

Enochian Tarot

Ishbel cards

Solomon deck of Priscilla Schwei

Ralph Blum's Rune Cards

Morgan's Tarot Deck

Masonic Tarot

Haindl Tarot

These represent only a tiny fraction of the total number of decks available.

Naturally, I do not keep every single deck in a special box wrapped in a consecrated cloth.

That is only for the one deck you use for some particular, special purpose.

The next question is, where can I buy Tarot decks? Most book stores carry one or two of the more popular decks such as the Rider/Waite. Beyond that, you will have to visit an occult/ New Age/magical book store. Most large cities have one or more of these. There are also mail order firms such as Pyramid Books of Salem, Massachusetts, that carry a variety of Tarot decks. You can also buy them direct from the publisher. Several are available from Llewellyn (see Llewellyn's *New Worlds of Mind & Spirit*— call 1–800–843–6666 for a free copy), including a few not published by Llewellyn.

A free catalog of Tarot cards (and another one of regular playing cards) published by U.S. Games Systems, Inc., is available from them at 179 Ludlow Street, Stamford, Connecticut 06902, or call 1–800–544–2637. Good collecting!

On the following pages you will find listed, with their current prices, some of the books now available on related subjects. Your book dealer stocks most of these and will stock new titles in the Llewellyn series as they become available. We urge your patronage.

TO GET A FREE CATALOG

To obtain our full catalog, you are invited to write (see address below) for our bi-monthly news magazine/catalog, *Llewellyn's New Worlds of Mind and Spirit*. A sample copy is free, and it will continue coming to you at no cost as long as you are an active mail customer. Or you may subscribe for just $10 in the United States and Canada ($20 overseas, first class mail). Many bookstores also have *New Worlds* available to their customers. Ask for it.

TO ORDER BOOKS AND TAPES

If your book store does not carry the titles described on the following pages, you may order them directly from Llewellyn by sending the full price in U.S. funds, plus postage and handling (see below).

Credit card orders: VISA, MasterCard, American Express are accepted. Call us toll-free within the United States and Canada at 1-800-THE-MOON.

Postage and Handling: Include $4 postage and handling for orders $15 and under; $5 for orders *over* $15. There are no postage and handling charges for orders over $100. Postage and handling rates are subject to change. We ship UPS whenever possible within the continental United States; delivery is guaranteed. Please provide your street address as UPS does not deliver to P.O. boxes. Orders shipped to Alaska, Hawaii, Canada, Mexico and Puerto Rico will be sent via first class mail. Allow 4-6 weeks for delivery. **International orders:** Airmail – add retail price of each book and $5 for each non-book item (audiotapes, etc.); Surface mail – add $1 per item.

Minnesota residents add 7% sales tax.

Llewellyn Worldwide
P.O. Box 64383-791, St. Paul, MN 55164-0383, U.S.A.

For customer service, call (612) 291-1970.

Prices subject to change without notice.

THE HEALING EARTH TAROT KIT
**A Journey in Self-Discovery,
Empowerment & Planetary Healing**
Jyoti and David McKie

The Healing Earth Tarot Kit offers a fresh visual way to access intuitive guidance. The beautifully illustrated pack of 105 cards includes new images, suites and spreads to deal with contemporary questions and conditions, and it revitalizes those parts of the traditional tarot most relevant to today. The Healing Earth Tarot draws together teachings from many ancestors and many lands (including Aboriginal, African, Celtic and Native American) to reveal how our health and the earth's health interweave into the same web of power. Used with the accompanying book, which explains in simple terms how to consult and interpret the images, the cards may be drawn individually for daily guidance or laid out in appropriate spreads. Their clarity and beauty enable you to access your own inner knowing and ask for help with any aspect of your life. Each unique image has a message designed to empower you to make both everyday and momentous life decisions.

Most of the major arcana cards are presented in a new light, with several of their names altered to emphasize concern for higher awareness in ourselves. The Hermit, for example, become The Wise Old Woman and reinstates the feminine wisdom hidden deep within ourselves. The Magician has become The Shaman in the ancient tradition of wisdom and healing.

A tarot now emerges which expresses the balance of male and female, the rehonoring of our elders, and the bridge between ancient and modern ... one which can help us integrate our sensitivity, in terms of psychic and spiritual depths, by the power of the heart ... a tarot which reflects our earth community and its diversity and which points the way to healing the earth through healing the self.

Book: 5 ¼ x 8, 288 pp., softbound • illus • index
Deck: 105 cards
1-56718-454-5 $34.95

Prices subject to change without notice.

ROBIN WOOD TAROT DECK
created and illustrated by Robin Wood
Instructions by Robin Wood and Michael Short

1 The Magician 1

Tap into the wisdom of your subconscious with one of the most beautiful Tarot decks on the market today! Reminiscent of the Rider-Waite deck, the Robin Wood Tarot is flavored with nature imagery and luminous energies that will enchant you and the querant. Even the novice reader will find these cards easy and enjoyable to interpret.

Radiant and rich, these cards were illustrated with a unique technique that brings out the resplendent color of the prismacolor pencils. The shining strength of this Tarot deck lies in its depiction of the Minor Arcana. Unlike other Minor Arcana decks, this one springs to pulsating life. The cards are printed in quality card stock and boxed complete with instruction booklet, which provides the upright and reversed meanings of each card, as well as three basic card layouts. Beautiful and brilliant, the Robin Wood Tarot is a must-have deck!

0-87542-894-0, boxed set: 78-cards with booklet

$19.95